Grading Strategies for the Online College Classroom:

A Collection of Articles for Faculty

MAGNA

Madison, Wisconsin

Magna Publications
2718 Dryden Drive
Madison, WI 53704
Magnapubs.com

ISBN: 978-0-912150-56-7

Contents

Foreword

One of best ways instructors can support students' success in online environments is through clear and frequent communication, but when it comes to the subject of grading practices, many of us are so focused on merely managing our grading that we neglect to consider the many ways grading can improve student learning. In fact, when we focus on grading practices as a facet of classroom management instead of a part of our course design that can engage and encourage our students, we miss key opportunities to retain and remediate struggling students and to further connect with the students who are already engaged and working well.

If online instructors began to view grading practices as a way to communicate clear expectations for students, promote multiple means of assessment, and encourage students' increased participation in the online classroom, we might begin to incorporate creative alternatives that allow for more purposeful interactions with our students and more continuous communication that leads to student retention and satisfaction in our courses.

How would that change our attitudes about grading—and students' attitudes about receiving grades? What immediate steps could we take to begin this shift from working on grades to having grades work for us—and for our students?

Grading Strategies for the Online College Classroom: A Collection of Articles for Faculty answers these questions and is an essential resource for instructors teaching courses in an online environment. In this collection, dozens of seasoned instructors across the disciplines share their best practices for online assessment, including how to design practical and meaningful assessment tools, how to evaluate participation to encourage online interaction, how to write feedback and use grading techniques that work well in online classes, and how to include authentic, clear, and purposeful communication to support grading strategies in online courses.

Each chapter focuses on a specific area of grading strategies with an array of assignment and assessment ideas that can be immediately and easily implemented in instructors' courses. "Exams and Quizzes in the Online Classroom" opens with online assessments and how they differ—and need to be different—from those in the face-to-face classroom. Building on the premise that online assessments are best when they are low stakes and encourage exploration of a topic, the chapter offers a series of practical options for how to uniquely assess learners' knowledge in online environments. In this chapter, instructors new to teaching online who may be interested in moving a traditional course into an online space will learn various ways to assess students' mastery in the new classroom environment, and experienced instructors will glean new ideas about alternatives to traditional testing and ways to improve existing assessments in their courses.

"Grading Participation in the Online Classroom" lays the groundwork for purposeful, organized discussion-based assessments that work for instructors *and students* by encouraging instructors to have clear course design in this area and providing key strategies for designing and evaluating online discussions that get students involved and engaged in the learning process. This chapter goes beyond conventional discussion boards and suggests using social media alternatives that meet students where they are and being more creative with policies about discussions so that students are encouraged to start talking and keep talking.

"Feedback and Grading Techniques for the Online Classroom" illuminates the many opportunities for creative and unconventional assessments that engage students effectively. In addition to practical recommendations about how to manage grading in larger online classrooms, the chapter provides readers with suggestions about how to implement collaborative assignments that enrich students' experiences and lighten instructors' grading loads. From analytics to Google tools, from clickers to comment archives, this chapter's resources will equip and inspire instructors at every level of experience.

"Communication Strategies for the Online Classroom" suggests ways that instructors can make expectations for students more transparent and can put students at ease with clear and consistent communication within the online classroom. With detailed guidance on rubrics, active learning, and podcasting, these articles present instructors with a variety of opportunities to connect meaningfully with students so that they get engaged and stay engaged throughout the course.

As accessible as it is comprehensive, *Grading Strategies for the Online College Classroom* serves its readers well as an easy reference guide to best practices in online education. Written and designed by educators with online faculty in mind, *Grading Strategies for the Online College Classroom* will challenge readers to reflect critically on their current grading strategies, inspire them to consider changes to promote student engagement and success, and prepare them with the tools and ideas to begin today.

Deidre Price, PhD
Northwest Florida State College

CHAPTER 1

•

Exams and Quizzes in the Online Classroom

Online Quiz Formats: Do They Matter?

by Maryellen Weimer, Penn State Berks

Use of online quizzing continues to grow. If taken online, quizzes don't consume valuable class time. Grading occurs automatically and doesn't consume valuable teacher time. Students get feedback immediately. The technology also offers a variety of format options. But do we know anything about how these various quiz formats affect learning? We don't know much, and so far, the research offers an array of mixed results. But a recent study finds that format does make a difference

Students in this study (a sizable cohort) were enrolled in one or two semesters of an introductory undergraduate physiology course at the University of New South Wales. Starting in 2009 a quizzing component was introduced in the course, and during the next three years it was used in four different formats:

1. Three quizzes, each worth 5 percent of the grade, taken without supervision, with the use of notes and textbook discouraged, each 10 questions and each completed in 20 minutes with only one try
2. Three quizzes, each worth 5 percent of the grade, taken with supervision, no books or notes permitted, each with 10 questions and each completed in 20 minutes with only one try
3. Two quizzes, each worth 7.5 percent of the grade, taken with supervision, no books or notes, each with 15 questions and each completed in 30 minutes with only one try
4. Five quizzes, each worth 2 percent of the grade if the score was higher than 90 percent, taken without supervision, open book, with more questions, no time limit and unlimited tries

"Cohorts of students undertaking the courses in which quizzes were offered in the format of models 1–3 did not demonstrate any significant overall improvement in learning outcomes as measured by performance in the summative end-of-session examinations. In contrast, the implementation of quizzes in the format of model 4 ... was associated with a significant improvement in mean summative end-of-session examination scores" (Marden 2013, 196). The research team offers this larger conclusion at the end of the article: "Our study supports the notion that in order for online formative assessments to be effective, they must be perceived by students to be relatively low stakes and allow exploration of existing and expected knowledge in a nonthreatening environment" (Marden 2013, 199).

There was also a strong correlation between quiz scores obtained in all four formats and scores on the final exam. Students who did well on the quizzes did well on the final, and students who did poorly on the quizzes did poorly on the final exam, often failing it. On the basis of this correlation, the researchers suggest that teachers could use quiz scores to identify those students needing extra help and seek to intervene with them while there is still time for those students to make changes that could improve their overall performance in the course.

Students in these two sequenced courses appreciated the use of quizzes. Sizable majorities said the quizzes guided their study for the exams, helped them learn the content, provided feedback on their learning, and were challenging and valuable overall. A student who took the quizzes in format 4 wrote in response to an open-ended question, "Excellent revision tool. I would read over the lectures first, then attempt them first time under exam conditions—then redo them with material" (Marden 2013, 195).

Reference

Marden, N.Y., et al. 2013. Online feedback assessment in physiology: Effects on students' learning experiences and outcomes. *Advances in Physiology Education* 37 (2): 192–200.

Reprinted from *The Teaching Professor*, November 2013.

Creating Better Multiple-Choice Tests for Online Courses

by Patti Shank, learningpeaks.com

Multiple-choice tests are commonly used to assess achievement of learning objectives because they can be efficient. Despite their widespread use, they're often poorly designed. Poorly written multiple-choice tests are equally damaging in classroom-based and online courses, but in online courses learners often have to contend with more challenges, and poor assessments can add insult to injury.

Some plusses and minuses to multiple-choice tests

Multiple-choice tests can be developed for many types of content and, if the test items are well written, can measure achievement of multiple levels of learning objectives, from simple recall and comprehension to more complex levels, such as ability to analyze a situation, apply principles, discriminate, interpret, judge relevance, select best solutions, and so on.

Multiple-choice tests are easy to administer and can be improved using item analysis in order to eliminate or correct poorly written items. They are easy to score and less susceptible to scoring subjectivity than short-answer or essay-type items. They don't measure writing ability (which can be a plus or minus) and often do assess reading ability (another potential plus or minus, but in reality often a minus). They are more subject to guessing than many other types of learning assessments.

Multiple-choice tests are often promoted as objective. Although scoring them doesn't involve subjectivity, humans do judge what questions to ask and how to ask them. These are very subjective decisions!

When multiple choice is appropriate

Multiple-choice test items call for learners to select an answer or answers from a list of alternatives. Because they do not ask learners to construct an answer or actually perform, they tend to measure knowing about rather than knowing how.

Multiple-choice items cannot assess learners' ability to construct, build, or perform. They are best used for objectives that can be assessed by selecting the correct answer from a list of choices rather than supplying the answer or performing a task. Think for a moment about how different selecting is from constructing and performing and you'll recognize the limitations of multiple-choice testing.

Writing better multiple-choice items

Confusing and ambiguous language and poorly written or implausible distractors are very common errors when writing multiple-choice test items. Here's a to-do list to help you avoid these mistakes and write better multiple-choice test items:

- Provide clear directions. Group questions with the same directions together.
- Include as much of the question as possible in the stem, and reduce wordiness of alternatives.
- Include words in the stem that would otherwise be repeated in each of the alternatives.
- Make sure language is precise, clear, and unambiguous. Include qualifiers as needed, but don't add unnecessary information or irrelevant sources of difficulty.
- Avoid highly technical language or jargon unless technical knowledge and jargon are part of the assessment.
- Avoid negatives and these words: always, often, frequently, never, none, rarely, and infrequently. When a negative is used, it should be CAPITALIZED, underlined, or bold to call attention to it.
- Don't use double negatives or double-barreled questions (asking two things in one question).

It takes time and practice to write good multiple-choice questions. In the online space especially, where students may have even more challenges than in face-to-face classes, the time and effort put in to writing effective questions is well spent.

Reprinted from *Faculty Focus,* May 1, 2009.

Giving Math Tests Online

by Jennie Weber, Lake Region State College

When I began teaching online, I started with proctored exams. I was comfortable with proctored exams and believed that my students were too. However, many students had issues finding both suitable proctors and time to meet with them. For most students, online learning provides a way to juggle their responsibilities. Online testing just contributes to this. As one student told me, "I'm a mom of young children, and I also have a full-time job to support my family. Having tests online allows me to continue my education without having to compromise my ability to support my family or spend quality time with them." Another student said, "I've also had math classes where I have to print out the test, do pen/paper and then snail mail it back to the school. I do NOT like that option at all!"

The students are clear—online is their preference. Using proctors also meant allowing for mailing time and limiting the number of tests. When I moved to an online homework system, I decided to make the jump to online testing as well, something our online advisor had told me students often asked about when registering.

With the choice made to use online testing, I decided that I needed to revamp my testing procedures. To make this a mutually beneficial move, I made several adjustments to my assessment procedures.

First, tests and quizzes would be open note/book. The reason is simple: there is no way to monitor what students are doing; therefore, it was better to adjust accordingly ahead of time. I made two basic changes to my exams and quizzes. First, I increased the difficulty of the exams, since I knew they had notes. Second, I set strict time limits to make sure they were not just looking up every problem. I did create for the students an information sheet on taking online tests, so they knew what to expect and to encourage proper preparation. Among the suggestions were basic ideas, such as making truncated notes, marking up their books, and organizing all their materials for easy access. In other words, they would have to study hard in the process of creating all these prepared materials so they would be ready for the test.

Second, I would give students the option of sending in their scratch work for partial credit. The students have to scan/fax their handwritten materials to me after taking the test or quiz. One of my statistics students reported, "I also like being able to use pen/paper to work out a problem. Some of my past tests have allowed me to add attachments when submitting my tests. Other systems don't allow this, and I have to manually email to the instructor." This requires the students to take the initiative, but most students who do this see a nice jump in their grades. Since the online test bank I use is mostly multiple-choice problems (I do write problems myself if there is something not available that I want, but I like the ease of their algorithmic, randomized problems, which help combat cheating), there was no way to give partial credit without this addition.

Third, with the ease of online testing, I was able to add quizzes to my syllabus, and I am now working to add more tests. Research shows that more testing improves student retention, and the more students are forced to review the material, the better. (An example of this research is H.L. Roediger and J.D. Karpicke, "Test-enhanced learning: taking memory test improves long-term retention," *Psychological Science* 17 (3): 249–255.) With the time constraints of proctored exams, I was hesitant to add more tests; but going online, I was able to make this transition.

The quizzes are meant as test preparation, and I even drop a quiz grade to keep them low risk for the students. Every problem on a quiz is on the subsequent test (and I tell students this), giving them more practice and review. This also helps alleviate any computer issues that might crop up on the first test by forcing them to use all the tools early on. With many non-traditional students, taking a test on a computer can be daunting, so low-risk practice helps make them more comfortable before taking an actual test. As one student said, "The only thing I worry about is getting kicked off the Internet and not being able to get back into the test." This usually happens at least once on the first quiz, and my quick response helps alleviate any fears, as even without their seeing each other, word always seems to spread.

I have recently revamped my introductory algebra classes to include a test on every chapter and am working on similar revisions in my other on-line math classes. By giving more tests, I can cover less material on each, yet in much greater depth. The students also have less material to study, thus allowing them to focus on the material better. The tests are more representative of the entire homework set, so students really feel that everything they are learning is being evaluated. With the online system, I am easily able to coordinate homework and assessments so that they can be properly prepared by following my outlined suggestions.

In my first run of online testing, I noticed grades definitely went down. Students were not properly preparing for exams, assuming "open book" meant easy, and were not taking advantage of the option to send in work. This told me that the students were not preparing properly and needed more guidance. By overhauling my course as outlined above, I have seen a corresponding rise in test grades.

Overall, online testing has streamlined my courses. Going online has also allowed me to test more frequently and therefore improve retention of material and student success, so I see it as a successful move. As one of my statistics students wrote, "I prefer the online math tests as I feel I am in more control of the environment that I am testing in. … I also like that I can use scratch paper while still engaging in the exam online (the best of both worlds!)." With adjustments to my assessment procedures, I believe I am providing "the best of both worlds" to my students.

Reprinted from *Online Classroom*, December 2012.

Tests as Teaching Devices

by John Orlando, Northcentral University

Consider the following two ways to introduce an online lesson:

- In this module we will learn how gender differences are expressed in the traits of birds.
- Here are two photos of a robin, one male and one female. Tell me which you think is male, and why.

The first method puts the student into the passive, "getting lectured to" state of mind, while the second method forces the student to formulate a hypothesis about the subject. The student might guess that the male is the larger one because human males are generally larger than human females, and perhaps the same applies to other animals. The student might instead guess that the one with the darker coloring is female because she would be better camouflaged when nesting.

The student in the second case is applying their prior knowledge to the material. This is significant because we learn on the periphery of what we already know by connecting new information to prior knowledge. By formulating a hypothesis, the eventual answer gets connected to prior knowledge when the hypothesis is either confirmed or disconfirmed, thus building the student's overall knowledge base.

Opening with a question also piques the student's interest in the material. The student is now invested in the answer and will pay more attention to the material to see whether his or her guess was correct. This again improves retention.

A team of professors and instructional designers at the Cornell University Ornithology Lab used this opening for a biology class. Called "All About Fancy Males," the test presented students with a sequence of photos of male and female members of a bird species. Students were asked to pick out the male in each of the photos, and after submitting their guess learned whether it was right or wrong, and why. You can find it at: *biology. allaboutbirds.org/features/fancymales/fancy-males.*

Students started seeing general patterns in the correct answer over the course of the module, such as that the male was usually the one with the more elaborate coloring because that coloring is used to attract females. In that way they are learning fundamental biology principles through the test itself. The explanations would often include auxiliary facts, such as that the brighter coloring makes the male more visible to predators, thus increasing the importance of male health for survival. Some cases went against the general patterns, providing an opportunity to teach why evolution produces counter-examples. In one case the "fancy" trait was a behavior, such as a dance, which was demonstrated by a video.

Faculty generally think of tests solely as a means to assess learning after the fact. But tests can be used as learning devices themselves. They are especially powerful when used to provide immediate feedback. James Pennebaker and Samuel Gosling, professors at the University of Texas at Austin, experimented with adding daily online quizzes to their psychology class. Instead of having to wait until the end of the test to learn how they did, students were immediately told whether their answer was correct upon submitting it.

The results were striking. The students given the quizzes scored half a grade higher in the class than a group not given the tests. Even more interesting was that the quizzes produced a 50 percent reduction in the achievement gap among students of different socio-economic groups.

The reason for these results was most likely that frequent tests, along with immediate feedback, lead students to reflect on their learning, which has been shown to be a key to learning. Reflecting upon our learning improves not only our understanding of the immediate concepts, but our learning skills as well. This process is critical to self-regulating our learning. Unfortunately, we do little to teach students how to self-regulate their learning. Tests with immediate feedback can help serve this need.

Another method of turning tests into teaching devices is to add a "wrapper" around them (Paul 2015). The wrapper is a series of questions that students answer after the test about issues that might have influenced their performance. For instance, a test wrapper can ask students to list the amount of time they spent on different test-preparation activities, such as rereading class notes or working on sample problems. Students who do poorly on a test might see how different study strategies influence their performance, and thus adjust their methods accordingly.

The test wrappers can include questions about whether the student studies with music on, where the student studies, and the amount of time the student spends studying. This can lead students to think about how these other factors influence their performance.

Test wrappers can ask the student to reflect on why he or she missed certain answers on the test. The student provides an estimate as to the degree to which their problem is due to different factors, such as not understanding a concept, not being careful, and not being able to formulate an approach to a problem. This clues the teacher to the student's problems, providing a starting point for addressing them. By looking at class-wide patterns, the teacher can also identify common problems that require adjusting the course material.

Finally, the test wrapper can ask the student what he or she will do differently to better prepare for the next test. Students rarely reflect on how they will prepare for a test in the future. Asking a student to think about it and write down the answer can make a significant difference in their performance in current and future courses.

Learning management systems make it easy to add low-stakes tests to online courses. Consider how you might use them as learning devices before, during, and after students encounter the course content.

Reference

Paul, A. 2015. A new vision for testing. *Scientific American* 313 (11): 54–61.

Reprinted from *Online Classroom*, October 2015.

Seven Assessment Challenges of Moving Your Course Online (and a Dozen-plus Solutions)

by Emily A. Moore, Boise State University

Not all online courses are created from scratch. Many—if not most—are online versions of courses that have previously been taught face-to-face. In these cases, where an instructor or instructional designer is adapting an existing face-to-face course for online delivery, assessments already exist.

But to be effective in an online environment, the assessments that worked perfectly fine in a face-to-face classroom may need to be tweaked or even replaced. Why? Because the online teaching and learning environment presents the following seven challenges to traditional assessment implementations:

1. Cheating is easier to do (and harder to detect) online

While it's not clear whether online students do, in fact, cheat more than face-to-face students (Watson and Sottile 2010), the truth is that it is more difficult to monitor who's taking a test and how they're taking it online than it is in a classroom. Strategies for adapting assessments for online delivery include:

Timed/open book tests. Online, every test is an open-book test (except those that are proctored). To minimize read-as-you-go test-taking, reduce the amount of time students have to take the test so that only those students familiar with the material can answer the questions in the time allotted. Alternatively, replace selected response tests (such as multiple choice and T/F) with short-answer or essay questions that require students to apply textbook facts to novel scenarios.

Shuffled/randomized test questions. Shuffling questions helps reduce the likelihood that two students sitting in adjacent library carrels can take the same test together, one answering the "odds" and the other answering the "evens." Selecting questions randomly from a large test bank takes this idea one step further, providing each student with a similar (but not identical) assessment. (Most learning management systems provide both shuffling and randomization capability.)

Plagiarism detection software. Having students run their essays through a for-fee plagiarism detection service such as SafeAssign or TurnItIn can potentially deter cut-and-paste plagiarism. At the very least, it can start a conversation about how to cite sources properly.

Frequent low-stakes tests. Short quizzes or self-check activities worth no more than a few points each help make cheating more trouble than it's worth.

Performance assessments. Assignments that require students to write, speak, or present to the class are harder to fake—especially if they occur regularly throughout the course.

Coordinated tests. Instructors who teach multiple sections of the same class may want to coordinate tests so that all students take the same test at the same time. (Staggering tests increases the likelihood that the first students to take the test can pass on question details to their colleagues.)

Proctoring. Requiring students to take proctored exams takes cheating off the table—or, at least, returns it to the same level as a face-to-face class.

2. Online courses need more student-to-student interactions "built in" than do face-to-face courses

In a classroom setting, students interact—socially (chatting before class starts) and as part of common classroom activities (asking questions for clarification, weighing in on impromptu discussions, etc.) Online, these opportunities to feel connected and learn from each other do not occur naturally; they must be carefully planned and managed. Assessments that incorporate student-to-student interactions—while not appropriate for every course—can play a powerful part in a course's overall communication strategy:

Peer-review. Asking students to review their classmates' work (and grading them on their reviews) can help motivate best efforts as well as help students learn from each other.

Group projects. Well-designed group projects help students master both course content and team participation skills.

3. Online students need more student-to-instructor interaction than their face-to-face counterparts

While instructor interaction and feedback is important to all students, it's critical to the success of online learners and—like student-to-student feedback—must be carefully planned and cultivated in an online setting. Fortunately, online tools make incorporating student-to-instructor interaction into assessments relatively achievable via:

Frequent, low-stakes testing ("self-check" quizzes and activities). Options range from short selected response quizzes and watch-and-discuss questions to complex games and activities accessed through textbook publishers' add-on course cartridges.

Rich, detailed feedback. Strategies for providing rich, detailed feedback vary based on the activities you've selected for your online course. The most practical include building detailed feedback into selected response quizzes; actively managing discussion boards; and administering weekly surveys asking students to identify the concept(s) they're struggling with and then addressing the most-identified concept(s) by using a product such as Jing to create and post quick video clarifications.

4. Online students need more planned structure—that is, more help in staying on time and on task—than their face-to-face counterparts

The structure that occurs naturally when students and instructor congregate in the same place at the same time (seeing "Test next Tuesday" written on the white board, for example, or overhearing classmates a row over discussing an upcoming assignment) doesn't just "happen" in an online course; it must be planned and managed. These assessment-related techniques can help:

Frequent, low-stakes tests (ungraded or low-point-value "self-checks"). These help students gauge for themselves how well they're mastering the material.

Graded milestones. Breaking up large projects into smaller graded milestones helps students (and you) identify problems areas early enough to address them.

Graded participation. Using a rubric to grade discussion board participation is time-intensive, as is asking students to review each other's work. However, the benefits in terms of being able to gauge and guide students' understanding can often be worth the time investment.

5. Performance assessments (such as presentations and demonstrations) can be more challenging to administer online

Putting students "on the spot" in a classroom setting (by assigning them to demonstrate a process or deliver a speech to the entire class, for example) can strengthen their communication skills and help them learn from each other. Online, however, students need to be able to package their presentations so that their instructors and fellow students can view and provide feedback on them. Accomplishing this requires:

Low-cost/free hardware and software. Webcams and microphones are relatively affordable, and—given clear, step-by-step instructions—students can use free software (such as Jing, Screencast-O-Matic, or VoiceThread) to capture and distribute presentations. Students with access to iPads can use free/low-cost online services such as Educreations and Explain Everything to create and submit handwritten assignments (useful for math proofs, for example).

Free Web conferencing services (optional). With Google Hangouts, students can conduct synchronous presentations—useful for hosting live post-presentation Q&A sessions.

6. Students expect more visually rich and interactive materials delivered via screen than they do from an in-class experience

Face-to-face classes are inherently visual and interactive. In an online class, however, the amount and quality of visual and interactive materials can vary widely. To avoid turning an online class into an old-fashioned correspondence course ("read the textbook, take a multiple-choice quiz, and contact the instructor if you have questions"), online courses should incorporate as much rich, relevant multimedia as possible—including, where appropriate, interactive multimedia assessments such as:

Drag-and-drop activities. Consider replacing one or two multiple-choice quizzes with a drag-and-drop quiz that requires students to order or categorize concepts visually.

Image-based activities. For highly visual subjects such as art appreciation or biology, replace one or two multiple-choice quizzes with a series of images and require students to "click" their answers.

Audio-based activities. Consider requiring students to take assessments by recording their answers in an audio-only mp3 file format.

7. Because an online course typically takes more time to teach than the same course taught face-to-face, containing instructor workload with regard to administering online assessments is important

When students and instructor are in the same place at the same time, giving verbal instructions and feedback is easy and natural. Online, much of the feedback instructors give must either be written (via discussion boards, for example), which takes longer to compose; or it must be mediated through technology. Rather than hand-grade a math assignment and simply hand it back in class, for example, an instructor must either locate and learn how to use tools to mark up the digital version of the assignment, or mark it up by hand, scan and digitize it, and send it back to the student. None of these steps is particularly difficult—but the extra minute or two, multiplied by the number of students and number of assessments, can add up quickly (to say nothing of the additional time the instructor must spend teaching students how to hand in such assessments and dealing with the technical glitches that inevitably arise).

Strategies for containing the time required to provide feedback on assessments include:

Group projects. Having small groups of students work together to write a paper, create a presentation, or produce some other product assessment reduces the number of assessments you'll need to grade.

Peer-reviewed activities. Students post their work to a discussion board or a blog and then review two of their classmates' submissions. This strategy ensures all students receive valuable feedback while helping reduce the time the instructor must spend reviewing each submission.

Student-led discussions. Artfully guiding multiple discussion boards containing dozens of student participants is time-consuming. For selected discussions, organize students into small groups and assign one student to manage and summarize each small-group discussion.

Representative submissions. Using a multimedia tool such as Jing or VoiceThread to dissect, just as you would in the classroom, a few representative submissions (such as a research paper containing an ineffective conclusion and one that cites sources incorrectly) lets you address the most common problems efficiently, saving your remaining grading time for more personalized, in-depth student-to-student communications.

It's important to note that while implementation strategies differ in an online environment, the pedagogical strategies underlying assessments shouldn't change when you move a face-to-face course online. Online or off, assessments need to align with course objectives and provide a consistent measurement of student learning.

If having students hand-write math proofs so that you can assess understanding and grant partial credit makes sense in a classroom, for example, chances are it makes sense online, too. The pedagogical strategy (hand-written homework) stays the same; only the implementation strategy (having students create and sending handwritten work as a digital file) needs to change.

Reference

Watson, G. and J. Sottile. 2010. Cheating in the digital age: Do students cheat more in online courses? *Online Journal of Distance Learning Administration* 13 (1).

Reprinted from *Faculty Focus,* December 2, 2013.

Do Online Students Cheat More on Tests?

by Maryellen Weimer, Penn State Berks

A lot of faculty worry that they do. Given the cheating epidemic in college courses, why wouldn't students be even more inclined to cheat in an unmonitored exam situation? Add to that how tech-savvy most college students are. Many know their way around computers and software better than their professors. Several studies report that the belief that students cheat more on online tests is most strongly held by faculty who've never taught an online course. Those who have taught online are less likely to report discernible differences in cheating between online and face-to-face courses. But those are faculty perceptions, not hard, empirical evidence.

Study author Beck correctly notes that research on cheating abounds, and it addresses a wide range of different questions and issues. Faculty have been asked how often they think cheating occurs and what they do about it when it happens. Students have been asked whether they or their colleagues would cheat, given a certain set of circumstances. Students have been asked how often they cheat, how often they think their colleagues do, and whether they report cheating. The problem with much of this descriptive research is that it summarizes perceptions, what faculty and students think and have experienced with respect to cheating. And this in part explains why the results vary widely (studies report cheating rates anywhere between 9 and 95 percent) and are sometimes contradictory and therefore inconclusive.

Beck opted to take a different approach in her study of cheating in online and face-to-face classes. She used a statistical model to predict academic dishonesty in testing. It uses measures of "human capital" (GPA and class rank, for example) to predict exam scores. "This model proposes that the more human capital variables explain variation in examination scores, the more likely the examination scores reflect students' abilities and the less likely academic dishonesty was involved in testing" (Beck 2014, 65). So if a student has a high GPA and is taking a major course, the assumption is that the student studied, cares about the course, and therefore earned the grade. But if a student has a low GPA and doesn't care about the course and ends up with a high exam score, chances are the student cheated. It's an interesting method with a good deal more complexity than described here. .

The study looked at exam scores (midterms and finals, all containing the same questions) of students in three sections of the same course. One section contained an online unmonitored exam, another was an online hybrid section with a monitored exam, and the third was a face-to-face section with the test monitored by the instructor. In the online unmonitored section, questions were randomized so that each student received a unique test. Online students could not exit or restart an exam once they began taking it. The exam was presented to them one question at a time, they could not move backward through the questions, and the exam was automatically submitted after 70 minutes, the time allowed in the other two formats. Students in all sections were warned not to engage in cheating.

"Based on the results in this study, students in online courses, with unmonitored testing, are no more likely to cheat on an examination than students in hybrid and F2F courses using monitored testing, nor are students with low GPAs more likely to enroll in online courses" (Beck 72). Some had suggested that because students who had not taken an online course reported that they thought it would be easier to cheat in online courses, students with lower GPAs might be motivated to take online courses. There were only 19 students in the online course in this study, but across these three sections, GPA did not differ significantly.

Using this model to predict cheating, there was no evidence that it occurred to a greater degree in the unmonitored tests given in the online course. That's the good news. The bad news: "There is ample opportunity for cheating across all types of course delivery modes, which has been demonstrated through decades of research" (Beck 2014, 73). In other words, we still have a problem, it just isn't more serious in online courses, based on these results.

Reference
Beck, V. 2014. Testing a model to predict online cheating—Much ado about nothing. *Active Learning in Higher Education* 15 (1): 65–75.

Reprinted from *Online Classroom*, August 2014.

Testing What You Are Teaching without Teaching to the Test

by Cindy Decker Raynak and Crystal Ramsay

Have your students ever told you that your tests are too hard? Tricky? Unfair? Many of us have heard these or similar comments. The conundrum is that, in some circumstances, those students may be right. Assessing student learning is a big responsibility. The reason we report scores and assign grades is to communicate information about the extent of student learning. We use these indicators to judge whether students are prepared for more difficult work or ready to matriculate into majors or sit for certification exams. Ideally, scores and grades reflect a student's learning of a particular body of content, content we intended them to learn. Assessments (e.g., tests, quizzes, projects, and presentations) that are haphazardly constructed, even if unintentionally, can result in scores and grades that misrepresent the true extent of students' knowledge and leave students confused about what they should have been learning. Fortunately, in three easy steps, test blueprinting can better ensure that we are testing what we're teaching.

Step 1: Align objectives, assessments, and learning opportunities

Learning results from students' engagement with course content, not from the content itself (Light, Cox, and Calkins 2009). However, this is often not how we approach the planning of our courses. In our courses and lessons, we need to make sure that clear learning objectives drive the planning, that assessments are constructed to measure and provide evidence of the true extent to which students are meeting the objectives, and that, through the learning opportunities we provide students, they can engage with the content in ways that allow them to meet the objectives and demonstrate their learning. This is not a linear process—it is iterative, often messy, and shaped by contextual factors. Nonetheless, when alignment is a criterion for successful planning, we are more likely to be measuring what we're teaching. We do have to start somewhere, and a good place to start is with learning objectives.

Step 2: Write meaningful and assessable objectives

If objectives drive the assessments and learning opportunities that we create for students, then the objectives must be meaningful (Biggs 2003) as well as specific and measurable. The objectives are where we establish expectations for student learning. If, for example, we want students to think critically, our objectives must reflect what we mean by critical thinking. What we sometimes lack is specific language. Taxonomies (e.g., Bloom's Taxonomy, Anderson & Krathwohl 2001; Fink's Taxonomy of Significant Learning, 2013; Wiggins and McTighe's Facets of Understanding 2003; Biggs' Structure of Observed Learning Outcomes 2003) can be consulted to help craft the specific objectives to which we will teach.

We recommend crafting no more than 5–8 course learning objectives. The format of the objectives should follow this example: *Upon successful completion of this course, students will be able to evaluate theories through empirical evidence.*

Step 3: Create test blueprints

Designers of any major high-stakes exam (e.g., SAT, GRE, NCLEX) have to be able to claim that it tests what it purports to test. One way they do this is by building a test blueprint, or table of specifications. A test blueprint is a document, matrix, or other kind of chart that maps each question on an assessment to its corresponding objective, theme, or topic. If it doesn't map, it's not included in the assessment. A completed map represents how the items of an entire assessment are weighted and distributed across objectives, themes, or topics as well as how they are distributed across other important dimensions (e.g., item difficulty or type of question). A test blueprint is, essentially, a tool to help align assessments with objectives.

Course instructors also need to be able to assert that assessments provide evidence of the extent to which students are meeting the established objectives. If the blueprint doesn't represent the content that is being tested, adjustments should be made before administering the test. A test blueprint is easy to develop and flexible enough to adjust to just about any instructor's needs.

Consider the template below. The left-hand column lists—for the relevant chunk of content—objectives, themes, and topics. Column heads can represent whatever "other" dimensions are important to you. For example, in a political science course you could map higher level versus lower level items. Or, in a statistics course, you could map question categories such as recall, skills, and conceptual understanding. Once the structure of your blueprint is established, (a) plot each item with the numbers in the cells representing the numbers of items in each of the intersecting categories; (b) total the rows and columns; and (c) analyze the table and make sure the test will well represent student learning, given the objectives and students' learning opportunities for that content.

	Higher level question (as defined by the content and course level)	Lower level question (as defined by the content and course level)		TOTAL ITEMS PER OBJECTIVE
	OR			
	Recall of facts	Computational skills	Conceptual understanding	
Objective/ theme/topic #1				
Objective/ theme/topic #2				
TOTAL OF EACH "OTHER" DIMENSION				

As you develop the "map" of your assessment, consider these questions: What does each column heading mean? For example, what does "higher level" versus "lower level" really mean? Do you know? Would students know? Would student learning be improved if you shared the blueprint in advance? And, ultimately, will this planned assessment represent what you taught, what you intend to test, and how you intend to test it?

References

Anderson, L. W., et al. eds. 2001. *A taxonomy for learning, teaching, and assessing: A revision of Bloom's taxonomy of educational objectives.* Boston, MA: Allyn & Bacon.

Biggs, J. B. 2003. *Teaching for quality learning at university.* London: Open University Press.

Fink, L. D. 2013. *Creating significant learning experiences for college classrooms: An integrated approach to designing college courses.* San Francisco: Jossey-Bass.

Light, G., R. Cox, and S. Calkins. 2009. *Learning and teaching in higher education: The reflective professional,* 2nd ed. London: SAGE Publications.

Wiggins, G., and J. McTighe. 2005. *Understanding by design.* Upper Saddle River, NJ: Merrill Prentice Hall.

Reprinted from *Faculty Focus,* August 8, 2016.

Clarity and Consistency are Essential to Effective Online Grading

by Tim J. Bristol, Nurse Tim Incorporated

Using online tools in student assessment is an important strategy for today's faculty. These grading tools offer faculty and students many efficiencies and enhancements that allow for success and satisfaction in the assessment process. Online gradebooks allow for quick feedback in a logical format. Students can access their grades at their leisure. The online gradebook allows for connections between numerical grades and narrative feedback (e.g., instructor comments on a quiz). The gradebook can save faculty time in organization and communication to students.

Online quizzing is another area of efficiency and enhancement. These tools are usually available to most faculty, and can be used for graded and nongraded assignments. They can be administered in a face-to-face environment or fully online. When the tools include multiple-choice, true/false, and matching questions, the students can receive instant feedback. When essay questions are used, the instructor will not need to worry about lost papers and exams, as all are "locked" behind a password on a secure server. One final advantage of online exams is the item analysis that can be generated. Most online quizzing tools allow for instant item analysis reports that help faculty judge the validity and reliability of the exams.

Other online assessment strategies and tools that bring benefit to academia include the online discussion, online projects, and online group work. These tools allow for enhanced interactions compared to the face-to-face environment while building flexibility and realism into the curriculum.

Regardless of the online tool being used for assessment, two key principles must be addressed. These principles are clarity and consistency.

Clarity

Clear communications and guidelines are vital to the success of online assessment. The issues that drive the need for clarity are twofold. First, when online tools are used, there are different and sometimes fewer directional cues for the learner. These missing cues can be everything from handouts to facial expressions. When assessments are done online, there is a need to compensate for some of these cues. Compensation can come in the form of reminders in online announcements and emails. Other cues may come from online exam instructions and reminders in the stem of a discussion.

The second issue that drives the need for clarity involves adult learning theory. Adult learners come with many expectations of the learning environment. And since more adult learners are joining all academic settings, we are wise to consider their characteristics. Knowles, Holton, and Swanson (2005) discuss the fact that adult learners have a need for rationale and are quite motivated. This means that an assessment process that is confusing or poorly developed can cause them significant stress. This stress can adversely affect the assessment. In turn, this may lead to a bad grade and poor data for the faculty.

Strategies that can enhance clarity with online assessment often relate to verbiage. "Do the instructions make sense?" Ask an assistant or family member to read the instructions. If there are any questions, consider this a clue as to what students will experience. Another strategy is to "test-drive" instructions with students through a low-stakes event. For instance, have the online quiz be an in-class activity or extra-credit activity.

Clarity should be sought in all descriptions and steps in the process. In the beginning, some complexity may be left out of the process for the sake of ensuring that the first run is smooth. An example may be turning in papers digitally. The instructor has as an ultimate goal to have students attach a grading rubric to each paper before submitting both to the drop box. If this is the first time the instructor intends to use the drop box, consider skipping the requirement to attach the grading rubric. Save that for after the drop box tool has been mastered by faculty and students alike.

Another important part of developing instructions is the use of images. Images of the computer screen can be captured and pasted into the instructions. Using screen captures can clarify written instructions—when the instructions say "click the submit button" a picture of the submit button can be shown.

If these concepts seem difficult, ask a student helper to assist with image capture and edit. Student helpers have made my life a lot easier when it comes to technology.

As these tips demonstrate, there can be a lot of room for confusion when online assessment is used. However, once the initial foundation is laid, the benefits of online assessment can flow freely. To ensure that this flow continues, faculty will do well to pursue consistency.

Consistency

Consistency addresses the idea that students come to learn for the purpose of pursuing greater milestones in life. They do not come to learn about faculty preferences and quirks. Keeping this in mind, faculty need to look for ways to ensure consistency of instructional design between assessment strategies and within programs. This can apply to one's own course (i.e., the grading rubric for the concept paper is similar to or the same as the one for the final project). This includes consistency between courses as well. Are the discussion forum questions in psychology graded in the same way as discussion forum questions in sociology?

Consistency needs to be sought in terminology. Some courses will have the same assignment discussed in the syllabus, in the course calendar, and in the online course management system. In the beginning it may be difficult for faculty to remember to adjust all three when a change is made. However, this type of discrepancy can cause undue stress to weary learners who simply want to submit their papers before the deadline.

Within the department, consistency should be sought as well. In one liberal arts college, the grading rubric for online discussions is exactly the same in all the nursing classes. At another school, the education department has chosen to use one online testing package for all education courses. That group has also put policy in place that maintains consistency in the look and operation of the online course management system.

Summary

Clarity and consistency lead to a well-developed assessment structure. These concepts help to remove barriers to effective and efficient assessment. Once these barriers come down, satisfaction and sanity is enhanced for all involved.

Reference

Knowles, M. S., E.F. Holton, and R.A. Swanson, eds. 2005. *The adult learner: The definitive classic in adult education and human resource development*, 6th ed. Woburn, MA: Butterworth-Heinemann.

Reprinted from *Online Classroom,* March 2009.

CHAPTER 2

•

Grading Participation in the Online Classroom

* Not Addressed: Different Levels of student engagement w/ the course.
→ How do we make online class discussion a priority for the student?

Evaluating Online Discussions

by Maryellen Weimer, Penn State Berks

Discussions in class and online are not the same. When a comment is keyed in, more time can be involved in deciding what will be said. Online comments have more permanence. They can be read more than once and responded to more specifically. Online commentary isn't delivered orally and evokes fewer of the fears associated with speaking in public. These features begin the list of what makes online discussions different. These different features also have implications for how online exchanges are assessed. What evaluation criteria are appropriate?

Two researchers offer data helpful in answering the assessment question. They decided to take a look at a collection of rubrics being used to assess online discussions. They analyzed 50 rubrics they found online by using various search engines and keywords. All the rubrics in this sample were developed to assess online discussions in higher education, and they did so with 153 different performance criteria. Based on a keyword analysis, the researchers grouped this collection into four major categories. Each is briefly discussed here.

Cognitive criteria

Forty-four percent of the criteria were assigned to this category, which loosely represented the caliber of the intellectual thinking displayed by the student in the online exchange. Many of the criteria emphasized critical thinking, problem solving and argumentation, knowledge construction, creative thinking, and course content and readings. Many also attempted to assess the extent to which the thinking was deep and not superficial. Others looked at the student's ability "to apply, explain and interpret information; to use inferences; provide conclusions; and suggest solutions" (Penny 2009, 812).

Mechanical criteria

Almost 20 percent of the criteria were assigned to this category. These criteria essentially assessed the student's writing ability, including use of language, grammatical and spelling correctness, organization, writing style, and the use of references and citations. "Ratings that stress clarity ... benefit other learners by allowing them to concentrate on the message rather than spend their time trying to decipher unclear messages" (Penny 2009, 813). However, the authors worry that the emphasis on the mechanical aspects of language may detract from the student's ability to contribute in-depth analysis and reflection. They note the need for more research about the impact of this group of assessment criteria.

Procedural/managerial criteria

The criteria in this group focused on the students' contributions and conduct in the online exchange environment. Almost 19 percent of the criteria belonged to this category. More specifically these criteria dealt with the frequency of and timeliness of the postings. Others assessed the degree of respect and the extent to which students adhered to specified rules of conduct.

Interactive criteria

About 18 percent of the criteria were placed in this category, and they assessed the degree to which students reacted to and interacted with each other. Were students responding to what others said, answering the questions of others, and asking others questions? Were they providing feedback? Were they using the contributions of others in their comments?

This work is not prescriptive. It does not propose which criteria are right or best. However, it does give teachers a good sense of those aspects of online interaction that are most regularly being assessed, which can be helpful in creating or revising a set of assessment criteria. Beyond what others are using, a teacher's decision should be guided by the goals and objectives of an online discussion activity. What does the teacher aspire for students to know and to be able to do as a result of interacting with others in an online exchange?

Reference

Penny, L. and E. Murphy. 2009. Rubrics for designing and evaluating online asynchronous discussions. *British Journal of Educational Technology* 40 (5): 804–820.

Reprinted from *Online Classroom*, March 2013.

Facebook: Online Discussion Tool?

by Maryellen Weimer, Penn State Berks

Online discussion has become another strategy faculty use to engage students with each other and with course content. This method offers a safer way for students to participate, as they are able to prepare responses ahead of time and deliver them in writing. But online discussion tends to lack spontaneity. The exchanges are linear and do not reflect the give and take of a face-to-face conversation. Some research evidence is emerging (referenced in the article highlighted here) that students aren't all that enamored with online discussion. Only 7.9 percent agreed that "online discussion should be a part of college courses" (Camus et al. 2016, 85), and they reported that online discussions were not helping them learn.

Perhaps Facebook might be better than traditional learning management systems (LMS) "at encouraging student participation, fostering student learning, and increasing students' course performance" (Camus et al. 84). The authors of this study cite multiple references documenting that more than 95 percent of students have Facebook accounts. In September 2014, Facebook itself reported that 864 million of its more than one billion members access their accounts at least once a day.

But Facebook has not often been used as an educational tool and is certainly not perceived that way by students. It also has design features that offer some challenges to its use for online discussion; the authors specifically mention file incompatibility issues and privacy concerns as potential limitations. However, this research team found ways around the challenges they describe in the article and were able to compare "online discussions that took place on Facebook with those occurring on a traditional LMS . . ." (Camus et al. 2016, 85).

Online discussions in two different courses, Women's Studies and

Introduction to Philosophy, were studied, with comparisons across two sections of each course. The courses enrolled non-majors, mostly freshmen and sophomores. In both courses, the instructor posted prompts that encouraged application of course content to current events and counted participation as 8 percent of students' grade.

The researchers assessed student participation by looking at the total number of posts, the length of each post, and the type of post (e.g., a response to the instructor, a response to a fellow student, a response to a previous discussion thread, a response that prompted further discussion, etc.). To assess learning outcomes, they borrowed Fink's significant learning taxonomy, which includes dialog, application, and integration. Finally, they considered students' grades for participation in the online discussion and their final course grade.

Results were mixed. In the Women's Studies course, students in the Facebook section posted far more often—87.5 percent of the Facebook students posted 10 or more times, compared with 67.9 percent of the LMS students. Those using Facebook were more likely to make novel posts and to respond to other students, but they were also more likely to make "extracurricular" (unrelated to content) posts. Those in the LMS section of the Women's Studies course were more likely to respond to the instructor, write longer posts, and not post extracurricular content. In the Philosophy sections, students posted nearly equally on Facebook and the LMS (75 percent and 74.3 percent, respectively). Otherwise, the trends were similar.

[handwritten margin note: more posts, BUT more extra curricular posts]

As for learning goals, patterns were the same for both courses. More Facebook posts demonstrated evidence of peer dialogue, but in LMS exchanges, more posts showed evidence of integration and application. When evaluating performance, Women's Studies students in the Facebook section earned higher participation grades and higher overall course grades. In the Philosophy sections, grades were about equal for participation and for the course overall. Unlike Women's Studies participants, "the linear regression model examining factors predicting overall course grades in PHIL [Philosophy] exhibited very poor fit . . ." (Camus et al. 2016, 90). Engagement in online discussion in the Philosophy course was not strongly linked to overall performance in the course.

So, what's the better option for online discussions: traditional learning management systems or Facebook? "Put simply, the two environments are unique, each with its own features that encourage different norms of communication and behavior" (Camus et al. 2016, 90). The research team recommends that, "if the goal is to stimulate discussion and build community, Facebook is a good option. If the goal is to foster development of application and integration learning goals, then . . . LMS might be a slightly better choice" (Camus et al. 2016, 91). In choosing either, it's worth remembering what these results most clearly establish: "Different forums can affect classroom dynamics and student learning in different ways" (Camus et al. 2016, 84).

Reference

Camus, Melinda, et al. 2016. Facebook as an online teaching tool: Effects on student participation, learning, and overall course performance. *College Teaching* 64 (2): 84–94.

Reprinted from *The Teaching Professor,* June/July 2016.

Online Discussion Forums as Assessment Tools

by Ted Cross, Arizona State University

Classroom Assessment Techniques, or CATs, are simple ways to evaluate students' understanding of key concepts before they get to the weekly, unit, or other summative-type assessment (Angelo and Cross 1993). CATs were first made popular in the face-to-face teaching environment by Angelo and Cross as a way to allow teachers to better understand what their students were learning and how improvements might be made in real time during the course of instruction. But the same principle can apply to online teaching as well.

Impact and Examples

There are many types of CATs that work well in the online classroom. The KWL CAT stands for "What you Know, what you Want to know, and what you Learned" (Ogle 1986). Steele and Dyer (2014) found that KWL CATs increased student participation in online discussion forums. These authors implemented KWLs in their discussion forums and give the following example of how a KWL may be implemented:

Timeline: One week or module

Monday: Create and post additional question, "What we know," under DQ (Discussion Question) 1.

Example: "What do you know about a thesis statement?"

Wednesday: Create and post additional question, "What we want to know," under DQ 1.

Example: "What do you want to know about a thesis statement?"

Friday: Create and post additional question, "What we learned," under DQ 1.

Example: "What did you learn about a thesis statement?"

[handwritten margin notes:]
- what you know
- what you want to know
- what you learned

Wrap-up: On the next Monday, copy and paste a list of responses students shared relating to what they learned regarding the topic and objective. This is a choice opportunity to validate student learning and understanding regarding all the ideas they discovered. This type of positive feedback will help students continue to engage in future weeks and create a personal accountability for learning. This can also be an opportunity for instructors to reteach key points that the students did not pick up on or indicate in their "what we learned" post.

After implementing this style of CAT in the first half of their test classes and not in the second half, Steele and Dyer found an increase in the average number of student forum postings for those classes that used the KWLs over those that did not.

In my own study of CATs, my coauthor and I found that using simple practice problems as CATs in undergraduate math class discussion forums can be helpful. Several sections of 100-level math online classes were used as a test case. Half of the sections employed CATs that asked students to solve problems in the discussion forum and document their steps, and then discuss their solutions with their classmates and instructors. The CATs were simple postings of sample problems in line with the material from the week's unit. The students were asked to complete the problems in an open discussion forum where all students could see their attempts. In one version of the CAT, students were asked to document their steps. In all cases, students were encouraged to comment on each other's solution posts and to add correction and/or commentary. We later compared sections of classes that used these simple CAT interventions with those that did not, and found an increase in both frequency of student posting and subsequent mean quiz scores in the CAT sections (Cross and Palese 2015).

CATs are easy wins that can have a real impact in the online classroom, especially when used in the discussion forum space. These small checks for understanding not only deliver increases in participation and possibly learning outcomes, but can help us all adjust our teaching style or tools on the fly to better help students learn.

References

Angelo, T., and K. Cross. 1993. *Classroom assessment techniques: A handbook for college teachers.* San Francisco: Jossey-Bass.

Cross, T., and K. Palese. 2015. Increasing learning: CATs in the online classroom. *American Journal of Distance Education* 29 (2): 98–108.

Ogle, D. M. 1986. K-W-L: A teaching model that develops active reading of expository text. *Reading Teacher* 39 (6): 564–70.

Steele, J., and T. Dyer. 2014. Use of KWLs in the online classroom as it correlates to increased participation. *Journal of Instructional Research* 3 (1): 8–14. DOI 10.9743/JIR.2014.3.10

Reprinted from *Online Classroom*, July 2015.

Evaluating Discussion Forums for Undergraduate and Graduate Students

by Gloria P. Craig, South Dakota State University

The discussion forum is an essential part of online courses. It's where students interact, reflect, exchange ideas, and expand their knowledge base. The quality of the discussion forum depends on the ability to develop a sense of community, the clarity of the discussion questions, and the use of a grading rubric that includes standards of performance.

Sense of community

Cobb (2011) found that relationships, comfort, and community are important factors in undergraduate student success. She recommends establishing forums for student introductions, instructor involvement in the forums, and acknowledging students' points of view.

Mayne and Wu (2011)found that the following strategies increase student satisfaction with an online course and positively influence perceptions regarding social presence and group interaction: personal emails and biographical and personal information from the instructor, an introduction with specific course instructions, an inclusive syllabus with student and instructor expectations clearly outlined, assignment rubrics, links to helpful tutorials or resources, and an informal place for students to chat,

Another way to promote community is to provide a question-and-answer forum. This facilitates student exchange of information that does not require instructor input, enabling students to mentor one another.

Small group sizes (with no more than 10 students per discussion forum group) also can promote social presence and community. According to Schellens and Valcke (2006), small discussion groups have higher levels of knowledge construction than larger groups do. They also found that students want specific discussion forum guidelines and want the forums to be graded to enhance the level of responsibility.

Clarity of discussion questions

To be meaningful, discussion questions need to be correlated with the course readings and learning outcomes for each module. Students are more likely to understand learning outcomes that are directly connected with an assignment (forum, quiz, or paper).

Most discussion questions focus on the basic levels of thinking of Bloom's Taxonomy to evaluate students' understanding of the content in each module and their ability to explain ideas or concepts. Some questions may direct students toward higher levels of thinking, requiring them either to apply the information from the module to a workplace situation or to compare and contrast particular issues (analyzing). To promote higher levels of thinking, ask students to critique one another's posts (evaluating) and direct them to pose a question related to the topic of discussion (creating) to further stimulate discussion in the forum (Overbaugh and Schultz, n.d.).

In undergraduate courses, have students respond to the initial prompt and include rationale and references. Then have them reply to fellow students with substantial constructive feedback (remembering and understanding). Encourage students to respectfully consider the opinions of others, agree or disagree with those opinions, and provide rationale based on references or workplace experience (applying, analyzing). After all the students have posted and replied, post a closing post for the forum that acknowledges students' points of view, addresses any areas that need further clarification, and adds new content to augment understanding of the topic of discussion.

Hold graduate students to the same criteria as undergraduate students, but also have them include questions with their posts to further stimulate discussion. This leads to a higher level of thinking. Also consider requiring graduate students to handle their posts that include questions as individual forums. Have them take on the role of instructor, replying to other students and posting summaries for their forums (evaluating). The instructor would then read all the posts, including questions and summaries, and post a closing message as described above for undergraduate students.

Grading rubric with standards of performance

Use analytic grading rubrics for online discussions. Analytic grading rubrics have two major components: levels of performance and a set of criteria. Levels of performance can include terms such as *exemplary, proficient, basic,* or *below expectations* or can include numbers. Points can be attached to the levels of performance and distributed based on the total number of points allowed for a post in the discussion forum. Criteria depend on the learning outcomes for the course, but may include the following:

- Demonstration of an understanding of the topic of discussion through critical thinking, higher-order thinking, and uniqueness of contribution
- Community building through collaboration and connection with other students
- Proper netiquette and mechanics of writing
- Timeliness and participation with posts/replies

See my analytic discussion forum grading rubric for undergraduate students here and my graduate rubrics here.

Hold undergraduate and graduate students to the same standard in regard to netiquette, including language, spelling, and grammar, but modify the type and number of required references to suit the educational level. For example, undergraduate students may be required to include supporting references from their reading assignments, but Truemper (2004) suggested that the expectation for graduate students should be to include references from research journals.

The number of replies may need to be adjusted to suit the size of each discussion group. Typically, eight to 10 in a group is sufficient for a discussion that demonstrates interaction, reflection, exchange of ideas, and expansion of the knowledge base related to the topic of discussion. The number of points assigned to a discussion forum will also depend on the amount of responsibility assumed by the students. If students are required both to include a question to further stimulate discussion and to facilitate their forums by providing a summary, then additional points may be assigned to the discussion forum grading rubric. Last, the timeliness of the posts and replies can be negotiated with students, as many adult learners have busy schedules.

References

Cobb, S. 2011. Social presence, satisfaction, and perceived learning of RN-BSN students in Web-based nursing courses. *Nursing Education Perspectives* 32 (2): 115–119.

Mayne, L. and Q. Wu. 2011. Creating and measuring social presence in online graduate nursing courses. *Nursing Education Perspectives* 32 (2): 110–114.

Overbaugh, R. and L. Schultz. Bloom's Taxonomy. Retrieved from http://ww2.odu.edu/educ/roverbau/Bloom/blooms_taxonomy.htm.

Schellens, T. and M. Valcke, M. 2006. Fostering knowledge construction in university students through asynchronous discussion groups. *Computers & Education* 46 (4): 349–370.

Truemper, C. 2004. Using scoring rubrics to facilitate assessment and evaluation of graduate-level nursing students. *Journal of Nursing Education* 43 (12): 562–564.

Reprinted from *Online Classroom,* December 2013.

Online Discussion Questions That Work

by John Orlando, Northcentral University

Most online faculty know that discussion is one of the biggest advantages of online education. The increased think-time afforded by the asynchronous environment, coupled with the absence of public speaking fears, produces far deeper discussion than is usually found in face-to-face courses.

But many faculty undermine this natural advantage by crafting poor discussion questions. The number one mistake is to confuse a discussion question with an essay topic. *What are the three criteria used to judge whether patients are competent to make a medical decision for themselves?* is not a discussion question. It's an essay question and should be left to an essay assignment. I've also seen instructors turn discussion into research assignments by requiring students to cite a certain number of outside sources in order to get full credit.

I've come to believe that crafting good online discussion questions is just plain hard and instructors fall back on essay questions for lack of better ideas. Below are some question types that will help generate real discussion.

Case study

Case studies are an ideal way to illuminate practical consequences of different concepts. For example, in a medical ethics course I used the following:

> *A 72-year-old man is admitted to the hospital for a kidney transplant. His daughter is brought in as the best available match as a donor. As the man's doctor, you discover from the pre-op lab work that the daughter is not a suitable donor because she is not his biological*

daughter. What, if anything, do you tell the man, his wife, or the daughter?

This example provides an ideal way to explore how fundamental principles of privacy, physician honesty, and shielding a patient from harm collide in the real world. The question allows for a variety of answers, each of which takes the students deeper into the fundamental issues being taught in the course.

[handwritten: A good question allows for a variety of answers]

Controversy

Another good discussion device is to generate controversy with a statement that challenges common orthodoxy. Consider this question in an information security class:

> *A fundamental tenet of information security is that you must force the user to periodically change his or her password. But this practice actually undermines security. With constantly changing passwords, users are forced to write them down in an easy-to-find location or use an easy-to-guess algorithm (my street address followed by a '1,' then changed to a '2,' then changed to a '3,' etc.). We are better off letting users keep the same password indefinitely. Do you agree?*

Also important is that a controversial statement needs to draw a fine line that allows for reasonable positions on both sides of the issue. It's not helpful to say something patently outrageous, such as "Passwords should not be required at all." A good statement that challenges what is being presented in the readings demonstrates that the instructor considers the students co-investigators and allows them to draw upon their wider knowledge base to engage the issues.

Transfer

It's been argued that the highest form of understanding is demonstrated through transfer of principles to new situations. For example, I've taught the classic "Prisoners' Dilemma" (*http://pespmc1.vub.ac.be/PRISDIL.html*) as part of my ethics and political theory courses. If you are not familiar with it, the upshot is that there are situations in which the rational choice for each individual involved leads to a situation that is not optimal for anyone. Think of it as the "invisible hand" in reverse.

The concept was developed as a way to understand political structures, but once you understand the concept—really understand it—you find that a lot of ordinary situations are prisoners' dilemmas. I'm a bike racer, and I realized that bike races are examples of the prisoners' dilemma. So one type of discussion question is to demonstrate the application of a concept to an entirely different situation and ask students to generate their own examples. Students can then evaluate how well the others' examples illustrate the concept.

Summary

A good way to end discussion threads is to post a summary of the main points as well as your thoughts on them. Revisiting material is good for retention, and these summaries demonstrate that you are keeping abreast of the discussion. Alternatively, you can assign different students to post summaries of each discussion.

I like to do video summaries. Something about hearing a voice and seeing a face captures our attention. It requires only a cheap webcam and a few minutes of my time. Don't toil over getting it perfect—just speak your mind for a few minutes, and post it as a video.

Reprinted from *Online Classroom,* August 2013.

Generating Lively Online Discussion

by John Orlando, Northcentral University

Discussion is a critical component of any online course, but instructors are often puzzled about what makes some discussions lively and others dead. To fill this gap, He and Gunter examined the factors that lead to participation in virtual teams and came up with some principles that can help guide instructors in cultivating a robust discussion in online courses.

Reputation

People will share knowledge with others when it enhances their reputation. It is easy to forget that students who speak in class are speaking not only to the instructor but to their classmates as well. They are cognizant of how they appear to their classmates. Thus, they are less likely to take risks when there is an opportunity to be wrong in front of others.

So instead of asking questions with objective answers that can be wrong, or are the answers that the instructor has in mind, it is better to ask questions that allow students to express and defend their own views. In particular, questions that allow students to bring in their own experiences to illustrate a point provide an easy way to contribute without fear of being wrong.

Replies

Students are more likely to get involved in a discussion when they think that someone is reading comments, and replies are a measure of others' attention. Most online faculty require students to make one or more replies to other students in each forum, but they often forbid students to make simple "I agree" affirmations. While these signs of approval should not count toward a grade, there is no reason to forbid them. Just as we are encouraged by others liking our Facebook posts, students are encouraged by seeing other students approve of their posts, and so these signs of approval should not be discouraged.

Activity

Students are more likely to get involved in a discussion that is already active. Prior activity gives students more ideas for their own posts and demonstrates that others consider the topic interesting, which influences the students' own perception of how interesting the discussion is. One good way to preserve activity is to space out postings. Students might be required to make an initial posting on Monday or Tuesday and then reply on Wednesday or Thursday. The instructor can also set a regular schedule for adding his or her own comments. This gives the student a reason to periodically check in to get the latest updates.

Emotional bonds

Students are more comfortable participating when they feel an emotional bond of trust and comfort with others. This is what distinguishes discussions in an online course from the flaming posts on YouTube videos. The instructor can facilitate this bonding by requiring students to post a bio at the beginning of the course, and the instructor should take the lead by providing a bio for himself or herself. Students, and instructors, should be encouraged to make video bios—either using a webcam shot or "digital storytelling" format of narration over imagery—that better humanize them to others.

A Bio to make people feel comfortable

Task conflict

A discussion where everyone is just repeating what others say in different words is not interesting. Faculty should facilitate "task conflict," meaning disagreement about the task, not a personal disagreement, in order to generate interest. A discussion question might ask for positions on a controversial issue, one that allows for reasonable positions on either side. Of course, the faculty member needs to monitor the discussion to make sure that it does not slip into personal attacks, but fortunately this is rarely a problem in online courses. A boring discussion is more common than one with too much heat.

Leadership

While faculty normally set a minimum for participation, some people will naturally go beyond that and become leaders in the discussion. This is not a bad thing. These leaders can help seed the discussion with new ideas, and a group without leadership will have trouble getting going.

The trick is to avoid having these leaders monopolize debate and thus quash activity by others. Because there is no time limit to discussion, as there is in a face-to-face course, one person's posting does not prevent others from making postings. But too many postings by one person can create the impression of an unbalanced discussion. This can happen when one person seems compelled to reply to all others. Talk to anyone who seems to be monopolizing discussions, but understand that any group needs leaders, and so allow people to take leadership roles that help provide the nudge that gets discussion going. You can even reach out to individual students to ask them to take leadership on certain discussions, as a coach does with particular players. Students will generally feel complimented and respond positively when this happens.

Following a few simple principles will lead to exciting discussion in any online class.

Reference

He, J. and G. Gunter. 2015. Examining factors that affect students' knowledge sharing within virtual teams. *Journal of Interactive Learning Research* 26 (2): 169–87.

Reprinted from *Online Classroom,* April 2016.

Discussion Board Assignments: Alternatives to the Question-and-Answer Format

by Rob Kelly

If you're having trouble getting students to engage in the discussion forum, perhaps it's time to rethink how you use this tool. "Think of it as a place to foster interaction between the students through a variety of means rather than just asking them questions, although that's great too," says Chris Laney, professor of history and geography at Berkshire Community College.

Laney uses the discussion forum extensively in his online courses. Participation counts for 25 to 30 percent of the course grade, so the students feel that they need to participate. Rather than sticking to the question-and-answer format, Laney uses role plays, debates, and WebQuests to engage students in the content and with one another.

While some people may think that the discussion forum is not the appropriate place for these activities, Laney has good reasons for doing it there. He tried using a blog but found it to be "clunky," and the interaction was limited. "I feel that the discussion forum can be used for almost anything if it's thought of as an assignment feature rather than a question-and-answer forum. ... I'm very low-tech, so I don't find myself being drawn to a lot of the fancy gadgets every year that are supposed to make online learning better. I think it keeps [the course] manageable if students are not having to learn some new technical thing each time, spending all their time trying to figure out this new technology. Whether it's role-playing, debate, or a WebQuest, they're using the same basic technology."

Role-play

One forum activity, for example, asks students to do some research on a person living in an urban Roman city in the first century CE. Each student creates a character and writes a diary entry or letter recording what he or she did in the course of a day or a series of days. To do this well, students need to research a few things about the professions and classes that would have existed. "The students end up talking back and forth in character in a situation like that," Laney says. "At no point have I actually asked a question."

The key to making these role-play assignments work is providing explicit instructions. For each role-play assignment Laney provides about a page-and-a-half set of instructions, including background, lists of reading assignments, and a step-by-step explanation of what they need to do. Laney posts instructions within the discussion forum rather than in the syllabus or the course schedule, because the forum is where the assignment takes place and students are in the forum on a regular basis. Providing instructions in the forum instead of elsewhere also gives him the flexibility to make changes without diverging from the syllabus—the syllabus simply says that the forum continues from week to week and makes no mention of specific assignments.

Debate

Debates also work well in the discussion forum, Laney says. He recently had students debate whether democracy in the Middle East would result in better or worse relations with nations in the region. It's a pretty straightforward assignment; however, when having students debate it's important to set clear ground rules to keep things cordial and to avoid simplistic arguments.

The same notion applies to question-and-answer discussions. For example, he once had a discussion that asked students to compare the democracy of fifth-century Athens to the current democratic system of the United States. Which is more democratic? When he checked the forum the next day there were a bunch of messages such as "I hate George Bush" and "Obama's a socialist." "Then I [posted], 'This is way off topic. The main purpose of this assignment was to talk about Athens and learn about the Athenian system,' but by then it was too late."

Taking a lesson from this incident, Laney now includes a statement that says, "Note: The main purpose of this is to get a handle on the Athenian system of government, so please avoid judgmental comments about American politicians." "If I do that up front, I don't have redirect it a lot. We don't tend to get off topic," Laney says.

Discussion forums can also include audio. One of Laney's colleagues has students embed links to VoiceThread files they create to practice speaking in Spanish and critique each other's pronunciation.

WebQuest

In weeks when a major assignment is due, Laney gives students a less intense discussion forum assignment. Rather than carrying on a discussion over the usual two-week period, he has students do a simple WebQuest and post their findings without having to respond to each other. For example, he may ask students to post an image, video, or music clip from the Romantic Period of art in the 19th century and write a brief description about why it's considered an example of Romanticism.

Laney has good retention rates in his online courses—typically 75 to 80 percent and sometimes higher. He attributes these high retention rates in part to the discussion forum assignments.

Grading

To keep the discussion forum assignments manageable, Laney asks students to post their messages in a single thread. In a class of 25 people there may be 75 messages in a week, but having all the messages in a single thread makes it relatively easy to grade. "I keep up with it so I have a good sense of who's been participating actively and who has been sharing good information."

When a discussion forum activity is over, Laney can click on an individual student's name and at a glance assign a grade. It typically takes 30 minutes every two weeks to grade a 25-person discussion forum.

Reprinted from *Online Classroom,* September 2012.

What Research Tells Us about Online Discussion

by John Orlando, Northcentral University

Student discussion differentiates online education from the old correspondence courses. But there are still many questions to answer in order to facilitate good discussion online. Hong Zhiu, of the University of Texas at San Antonio, did a meta-analysis of studies of online discussion over the past 15 years and has interesting findings about participation. These findings can help instructors maximize the benefits of discussion.

A few students dominate

Studies show that a few students tend to dominate discussion, just as a few people tend to dominate face-to-face discussions. Yet, most students still talk more in an online discussion than in a face-to-face environment, lending evidence to the perception that online education tends to draw shy students out of their shells. This is one major advantage of online education, and a reason why discussion should be central to any online course.

The finding also reminds us that even in an online discussion, equal participation is not likely. While it is important to establish minimum requirements for participation, human nature means that some students will still dominate. In fact, trying to even out participation rates might have undesirable consequences, such as students posting just to meet the guidelines.

While we want students to learn how to express themselves, we might also consider the legitimate role of a "passive participant." Maybe that person is a good listener, while another who contributes a lot is a poor listener. The online instructor should ask whether the purpose of discussion is to get everyone to talk or to generate good ideas. If the latter, then craft discussion requirements to allow for discussion supporters who encourage others but do not take a larger role.

Participation between students increases over time

Studies have shown that initial discussion tends to be between faculty and students, but as time goes on, students start talking to one another more and more. This is encouraging, and the goal of an online course is to move the center of gravity of a class from the lecture to the discussion. The design of a traditional classroom with desks facing the instructor embodies the assumption that students are there to listen, and as a result discussion goes through the instructor. But everyone is in an equal position in an online discussion, so students tend to start genuinely speaking to one another.

This does not mean that online instructors should remove themselves entirely from discussion. Students want the instructor to be present, at the very least to demonstrate that students' points are valued. A good guideline is that an online instructor should foster, but not dominate, discussion. Provide the structure and initial nudge, but hope that it eventually gets taken over by students.

Constructive interactions

A third theme is that the majority of discussion is collaborative and constructive. Researchers found that responses generally contained supportive messages about others' postings. This is important, as people who do not teach online often assume that students will start flaming on online discussion boards. Flaming is context-dependent. Unlike in other forums, online students are not truly anonymous, and because the instructor holds the grades there is a built-in deterrent to flaming. Studies also show that responses to others were far more common in discussions than original postings. This again makes sense, as any discussion generally starts with an initial topic and then builds on that.

But the finding draws into question the common requirement in online courses that all students make an original posting. This can create multiple discussion threads that are hard to follow. Students will also run out of original ideas after a few postings are made, and turn their "original" postings into unoriginal comments.

Consider the purpose of the original posting requirement. It is to generate creativity? If so, then a response to someone else's point might contain more insight and creativity than an original posting. Maybe instead of requiring an original posting and one or two replies to others, just require one or two original thoughts.

The fact that most responses were supportive also raises the question of whether students are too nice in discussion. Some studies suggest that students are unwilling to challenge one another in discussion. Has the focus on acceptance and inclusion in today's education led students to be hesitant to disagree? The purpose of academic discussion is to model civil and constructive disagreement as a means of intellectual progress, and so an online instructor might deliberately "stir the pot" with postings that invite disagreement as a way to facilitate robust interaction and engagement.

Reference

Zhou, H. 2015. A systematic review of empirical studies on participants' interactions in internet-mediated discussion boards as a course component in formal higher education settings. *Online Learning Journal* 19 *(3)*.

Reprinted from *Online Classroom,* February 2016.

Determine What Students Know

by Rob Kelly

Depending on your teaching situation, you may or may not have the authority to design or modify a course. If you didn't design your course or have the permission to make changes, you still have the power to reiterate the lessons that you feel are most important or that students may not have understood the first time.

Students enter online courses with various levels of knowledge, experience, needs, and expectations. It's important to get a sense of what students already know in order to provide the appropriate levels of support and challenge.

The discussion forum provides an excellent opportunity to gauge students' knowledge levels. "If there's a discussion question that's very basic in week one of the course, I can interject some questions that jump ahead," says Michelle Manganaro, who teaches online education and communications courses at several institutions, including Massasoit Community College. "Maybe some or all of the students already know a lot of things coming up. It helps me benchmark what my other questions will be for the rest of the course. If they already know a lot of the terms, then maybe I can make the conversations more interesting and jump into scenarios that apply the material," Manganaro says.

More knowledgeable students may tend to answer questions promptly and thoroughly in the discussion board, leaving the others to think they have nothing to add. Rather than jumping ahead, Manganaro recommends backtracking, asking the knowledgeable student(s) to elaborate, provide examples, and simplify concepts.

Even though some students may have more knowledge on a topic, each student brings individual experiences that can add to the conversation.

Manganaro requires students to relate the discussion board topic to current events or personal experiences. In addition to improving the quality of participation, this technique also makes the content more relevant to the individual.

Before moving on to the next unit, Manganaro mentions the previous unit and gets benchmark assessments to ensure that students understand the content being covered.

Reprinted from *Online Classroom*, January 2015.

Encouraging Online Learner Participation

by Joan Thormann, Lesley University

Sustained, high-quality student participation usually doesn't happen on its own in the online learning environment. The instructor needs to model participation, create assignments that encourage it, and foster an environment that supports it. Here are some ways that I promote student participation in my online courses:

Use discussions as assignments

Rather than assigning an overall participation grade, I treat each one-to-two-week discussion as an assignment. The discussion assignment is typically tied to an independent assignment. For the discussion portion, each student reviews the work of one or two classmates and is required to post comments and/or questions. The independent assignment is worth 20 points and the associated discussion assignment is worth 10 points.

I find that students do not necessarily need much preparation to interact in these discussion forums after I model participation for them. I post substantive comments, and in my modeling I never have yes or no questions.

Create informal conversation spaces

The assignment and discussion forums are not the only forums in my courses. I have two other forums: The Coffee Shop and The Teacher's Room. The Coffee Shop is for students to engage with each other on topics other than the content of the course, which helps build community and makes students feel comfortable with each other. The personal relationships built there can carry over into the content-related forums, and I think this informal space helps make posting in all forums feel safer.

The Teacher's Room is for administrative issues and questions and comments about current and past assignments. I advise students to check this forum regularly for important information, and I encourage students to answer each other's questions there. Sometimes students will post additional resources or they'll bring up issues that aren't necessarily related to the current week, but they add to the learning experience.

Encourage and recognize go-getters

In each course there are typically two to four students (out of 15) who are real go-getters. They help set the tone of the course and can be very helpful in getting others to participate. I'll encourage their participation by sending them private emails saying something like "I really like what you had to say about _____. Thanks for contributing." I'll also recognize them publicly through an announcement in The Teacher's Room or an email to the entire class when I feel that a student has made an insightful comment about the course content.

Use student moderators

After I have moderated the discussion forum for three or four assignments, I turn moderating duties over to the students so that they become facilitators of the conversation, which creates a positive learning environment in terms of power-sharing, involvement, and ownership of the course.

Students can select which forum topic and week they would like to moderate on a first-come, first-served basis. The responsibilities are described in the instructions, and a week before they are to moderate I send out a reminder about their responsibilities, which include:

- Focusing the discussion on course content
- Encouraging new ideas
- Initiating further discussion through questions or observations
- Finding and communicating unifying threads
- Drawing attention to opposing perspectives
- Summarizing and posting a report about the discussion

I let the student moderators take the lead. I do not participate until the latter part of the week's assignment, but I do participate because it's important that the students don't feel abandoned by the instructor, particularly when the discussion is facilitated by a student who may not be very confident in the role.

An interesting dynamic occurs when students moderate. Students who either have moderated already or who will moderate in the future are very supportive because they've been in the hot seat or will be there soon.

Another wonderful quality of having student moderators is that they bring a different perspective to the course. I look at the content in a certain way. Student moderators—especially good ones—will often look at the content from a different perspective. They will raise topics that I would never have thought of talking about. They bring in different ideas—some do extra research to make sure they are well informed—and the conversation often goes off in impressive directions.

Students are usually quite positive about the moderating experience. When I survey my students, they typically say that moderating deepens their understanding of the content, that they enjoy taking on a leadership role, and that they see the benefit of having others' viewpoints brought to the forefront.

Reprinted from *Online Classroom,* August 2012.

CHAPTER 3

•

Feedback and Grading Techniques for the Online Classroom

Frequent, Low-Stakes Grading: Assessment for Communication, Confidence

by Scott Warnock, Drexel University

After going out for tacos, our students can review the restaurant on a website. They watch audiences reach a verdict on talent each season on *American Idol.* When they play video games—and they play them a lot—their screens are filled with status and reward metrics. And after taking our classes, they can go online to *www.ratemyprofessors.com.*

It may surprise us to think of it like this, but today's students grew up in a culture of routine assessment and feedback. Yet when they click (or walk) into our courses, the experience is often quite different: There are few high-stakes grades, big exams, or one-shot term papers. Despite critiques of high-stakes testing—Wideen et al. (1997) said such "examinations discouraged teachers from using strategies which promoted enquiry and active student learning [...] this impoverishment affected the language of classroom discourse"—teachers often still see "assessment as an index of school success rather than as the cause of that success" (Chappuis and Stiggins 2002).

Certainly, grades, when misused as what Filene (2005) calls a "pedagogical whip," can lead to problems: Grading curves pit students against each other, fostering strategic rather than deep learning (Bain 2004). High-stakes grading may contribute to grade inflation (Rojstaczer and Healy 2010). Grading pressures may even encourage cheating.

I offer the strategy/philosophy of frequent, low-stakes (FLS) grading: simple course evaluation methods that allow you to provide students with many grades so that an individual grade doesn't mean much. FLS grading can work in any course but is especially useful online, as it provides grade transparency for students and creates a steady information flow in an environment in which student-teacher communication is crucial to success. FLS grading can have several advantages:

- It creates dialogue. Frequent grades can establish a productive student-teacher conversation, and students have an ongoing answer to the question, "How am I doing?"
- It builds confidence. Students have many opportunities to succeed, and there is a consistent, predictable, open evaluation structure.
- It increases motivation. FLS grading fits into students' conceptions—and, perhaps, expectations—of assessment and evaluation: This is the culture they grew up in!

Some teachers may have an "allergic" response to the idea of giving lots of grades, but much "classic" pedagogical thinking (and writing) about grading predates both this culture of assessment and feedback and the teaching technologies now available, especially to online instructors. While some may resist grade-centric approaches, remember, in ideal teaching, perhaps *everything* is formative and you have small ratio, even one-on-one, interactions with students. Maybe there are even no grades at all. But such ideal environments are rare. We must give grades, so the issue is how we grade to the benefit of students.

The growth of online courses provides additional exigency for FLS grading. I'm always skeptical about those who privilege teacher-student interactions in onsite courses—how often do students talk to the instructor of their 200-student onsite lecture course?—but no doubt a key to effective online pedagogy is making sure you are *present* for students as their teacher. All students benefit from having a clear idea of their overall course standing, but we need strategies to provide online students with meaningful communications about the course, and what is more meaningful to students than clear grade data?

Frequent grade information also provides motivation, another especially important factor in online student success (i.e., see Schrum and Hong 2002). Frequent, immediate grade data should help students overcome the inertia of procrastination far better than that delayed reward of the grade far off in week 12.

FLS grading does mean that you will re-conceptualize the grading function in your course, and while FLS grading has a summative micro structure—sure, you give grades—the overall structure is formative. You can remove unproductive grading pressure, encourage intellectual risk-taking, and discourage plagiarism/cheating. And especially online, your overall response strategy will include this grade-based dialogue with your students.

You can still have your major papers and exams, but with FLS grading, a series of low-stakes assignments helps uncover points of intervention long before any high-stakes evaluation. Teachers are busy, but FLS grading can actually result in less work overall if done right, as *dialogue occurs through the grades*. For FLS grading, you will shift your course requirements, like this:

• Three big papers: 25 percent each • Exam: 25 percent	• Three big papers: 20 percent each • Exam: 10 percent • Informal work: 20 percent • Quizzes: 10 percent
• Two exams: 35 percent each • Final paper: 30 percent	• Two exams: 20 percent each • Weekly quizzes: 25 percent • Four short response papers/posts: 20 percent • Final paper: 15 percent

FLS is about feedback. Really, a high-stakes evaluation structure often precludes a feedback plan: You basically just provide summative evaluation. The meaning of "frequent" will vary based on your teaching style. At one time, I provided as many as five grades per week. I have shifted my approach, clumping various small assignments into one weekly grade so, each week students get one status grade, although I can break that down to individual assignments for them if asked.

I'll focus on two particular assignment methods: informal writing and quizzes.

- Frequent short, informal writing assignments can take many forms:
- Responses to readings or focused content questions
- End-of-unit notes on important or confusing points, questions
- Journals
- Brief annotations or notes about calculations, charts, tables
- Metacognition: Have students think through/reflect on reasoning, thinking, writing processes

The technological environment of online learning is a major asset in using short, informal writing. Technology reduces the paper shuffle, easing logistics, and digital writing forums and tools allow students to write to one another, making open dialogue a fundamental course component. Message boards are an easy-to-use and readily available dialogic technology for online courses, and blogs or even wikis can be used to replace notebook-based response journals.

Rubrics provide structure for responding to writing and demystify evaluation— for you as well as the students. A simple rubric for brief informal writing could involve two simple criteria, on a scale of 1–5:

- Demonstration of understanding of a key idea
- Writing quality (judged loosely, maybe even as your readerly response to the piece)

When developing a rubric, remember what you want the assignment to accomplish. This is *your* decision based on your course goals. Don't outsmart yourself. In line with writing across the curriculum approaches, remember what you're trying to accomplish when you assign informal writing, and remember what you *don't* want to worry about. You do *not* need to evaluate everything. For instance, if you want to evaluate their understanding of a main idea about a chapter but end up pegging them for dangling modifiers, you will likely become frustrated and may give up on using informal writing at all. Think about simple, specific, often content-oriented goals you want to assess. Rubric performance language/levels can be simple, excellent to poor, and reflect a range of responses. You can use rubric creation tools like Waypoint Outcomes or Rubistar.

Quizzes need not be a pedagogical stick. Quizzes should be easy to create, take, and grade. They should have a specific objective. For instance, I always give straightforward, weekly online reading quizzes, *almost* at this level: "What large sea mammal is featured in *Moby Dick*?" I just want them to read.

Technology again simplifies logistics, easing both assignment submission and grading. Course management system (CMS) assessment tools allow for simple quiz features like question sets so not all students receive the same questions, and I use the basic simplicity, frequency, and low-stakes aspects of my quizzes to discourage cheating.

The primary question most teachers have is this: How do I give lots of grades without breaking my back? Again, use a simple grading scale for individual assignments: 1–3, 1–5, 1–10, or even a check/check plus system. You can share/display grades in a CMS grade book. Remember, the object is creating grade-centric feedback, and the time payback comes when students do not constantly have to reach out to you about class performance; they already know, and when they do raise questions, the conversation is more focused than, "So, how am I doing in this class?"

Filene (2005) said, "For better or worse, grades matter; the challenge is how to make them work for your purposes." FLS grading can demystify course assessment, letting your online students know how they are doing. Done right, it can result in less work/stress for teachers, helping identify struggling students early. Communicating meaningfully with every student is a teaching challenge, but a stream of FLS grades allows student to know where they stand so they can better reach their goals in our courses.

References

Chappuis, S. and R. Stiggins. 2002. Classroom assessment for learning. *Educational Leadership* (September): 40–43.

Bain, K. 2004. *What the best college teachers do.* Cambridge, MA: Harvard University Press.

Filene, P. 2005. *The joy of teaching.* Chapel Hill, NC: University of North Carolina Press.

Rojstaczer, S. and C. Healy. 2010. Grading in American colleges and universities. *Teachers College Record* (March 2010): http://www.tcrecord.org.

Schrum L. and S. Hong. 2002. Dimensions and strategies for online success: Voices from experienced educators. *Journal of Asynchronous Learning Networks* 6 (1): 57–67.

Warnock, S. 2004. Quizzes boost comprehension, confidence. *The Teaching Professor* 18 (3): 5.

Wideen, M.F. et al. 1997. High-stakes testing and the teaching of science. *Canadian Journal of Education* (22) 4: 428–44.

Reprinted from *Online Classroom*, March 2012.

Designing Collaborative Learning Experiences That Prepare Students to Work in Virtual Teams

by Lori Weir, Middlesex Community College

Another awkward group project: Does this sound familiar? It's the week you roll out the group project in your online course. You're watching the discussion board and the email trails. In each group, a student cautiously emerges as the discussion leader—you can tell that he or she doesn't want to appear controlling, but is eager to begin. One or two other students check in and dutifully reach out to the rest of the group, hoping to hear from their partners, but are not really invested in the possibility of a reply. Some students don't jump in at all. And so it goes . . . Not only do your spirits sag as you preside over another uninspiring group project, but you are increasingly concerned about students' abilities to effectively navigate collaborative projects in their future workplace.

I have been requiring a group project in my online course for about five years now because I recognize the value of collaborative learning experiences. To create plausible workplace scenarios, I paired students up and provided assignment guides and rubrics. I assessed them on their group's ability to determine the scope of the project, assign tasks for each group member, make decisions collaboratively, and include appropriate content.

At the start of each semester, I'd find myself tweaking the project because something about it never seemed to work. I would change the timing, varying the point within the semester at which the project was rolled out; I would alter the way I grouped the students; I would modify the deliverables. But I never felt the assignment was a success. The truth is, I disliked this part of the semester, and although I had a rubric, it wasn't clear to me that the students were learning much from the experience. Never once had a student contacted me to say that he or she enjoyed the project or that it had been in any way worthwhile.

A fatal flaw in the design

After trying the same things over and over and getting the same results, I finally took a step back and put on my instructional designer's hat. Here is what I discovered: The group projects failed because I simply had not built the students' capacity for group work. Regardless of where I placed the project within the calendar, I hadn't given students the chance to build rapport with one another, or with me as the facilitator and key stakeholder. I had provided neither instruction for working in teams nor any practical strategies for exercising communication skills, and the only tools the students had for communicating were a discussion board and emails. I asked myself, "In the 'real world,' who does an entire project—from initiating to closing, and with people they've never met—exclusively via email?" It was a bad design, and once the weaknesses were evident, I warmed to the challenge of designing a group project that delivered the learning value I knew was possible.

Back to basics

First, I had to clarify my purpose for including a group project. What were the intended outcomes—communication skills? Collaboration skills? If this was to be more than just an obligatory group project, if I was going to claim fostering these skills as an outcome, I had to design with a sense of purpose. I had to have a clear plan for teaching and assessing specific skills. If I wanted the *group* to work as a *team,* I had to offer direct instruction and ample opportunity for students to apply the principles in context. Essentially, the project had to be everything that my earlier iterations were not.

To build capacity, I had to
- build student rapport and minimize the transactional distance between members of the class;
- offer students guidance for working in groups and teams; and
- equip students with the technical means to complete the project.

At this point, my head was swirling with several ideas. To organize my thoughts, I pulled out my copy of Wiggins and McTighe's *Understanding by Design* (1998), and followed their backwards design process to "identify desired results, determine acceptable evidence, and plan learning experiences and instruction" (McTighe and Wiggins 1998, 9).

Identify desired results

What should students know, understand, and be able to do at the conclusion of the group project? I saw a three-pronged mission: The exercise should help students reinforce and synthesize course content, learn about the technical and social aspects of using new technologies, and strengthen the interpersonal communication skills necessary for working in groups and teams.

I already had a good sense of what student progress would look like in the first two of these outcomes. Measuring students' mastery of interpersonal communication skills, on the other hand, posed more of a challenge. Obviously, the full range of skills needed to communicate effectively and productively with a work team cannot be fully developed in a 15-week online course: "Indeed, it takes a lifetime for an individual to reach his or her potential as a leader and team member" (Carr et al. 2005, 3). Mindful of the constraints I faced in measuring lasting behavioral change, I did a good deal of research and eventually settled on a statement of acceptable evidence for this, the most challenging of my three desired outcomes: "Students should demonstrate the ability to utilize strategies and techniques that are essential for effective interpersonal communication in business, within groups and teams." The strategies I specifically targeted were active listening and responding, giving and receiving feedback, and resolving conflict.

Determine acceptable evidence

How would I know if a student reached this goal? I considered my options and decided that assessment could be made in a number of ways: observation of collaborative learning experiences, as posted in the debriefs on the student discussion board; self-reflections in individual accounts that students would keep throughout the team project; and the self-, peer, and team evaluations that students would complete at the end of the project. I would be looking to see evidence of six to eight situations in which a student identified a communications opportunity and either employed a strategy or realized in hindsight that a particular strategy would have better served him or her. I wasn't expecting exactitude, but rather that students could demonstrate an ability to call upon strategies that made sense in the situations they encountered.

Plan learning experiences and instruction

The next question was, how would this unfold? To plan the learning experiences and instruction, I created a graphical timeline of the course, which provided a bird's-eye view of how much time I had to build capacity, how much time I could allot for the project, and where I needed to focus solely on content. I decided the project would span five weeks and would encompass two stage theories: Bruce Tuckman's "Stages of Team Development" and the Project Management Institute's "Five Process Groups of Project Management." With two weeks allotted at the end of the course, this left me roughly eight weeks leading up to the project to prepare students.

At this juncture, I weighed my options regarding which tools to adopt. I wanted the activities to be authentic and relevant, so I adopted tools students would see outside of the college classroom: Twitter, Skype, and GoogleDocs (I've also since used Windows Live). I envisioned Twitter's platform as a place to build community. Skype's video feature would minimize the transactional distance by allowing students to hear and see one another. Finally, GoogleDocs would provide students with a platform for creating, storing, and sharing documents. In addition to the technology, and equally important, I carefully selected articles that offered techniques and proven strategies for the communication skills I aimed to target and the outcomes I intended to achieve.

Summary

By incorporating these tool-based interactive exercises in the first part of the course, I set the stage for successful collaboration in a way that my earlier project designs had missed. Student comments following the newly designed course offer evidence that not only have the inherent flaws with the earlier projects been fixed, but students feel that the project is a worthwhile learning experience. By adding rapport-building activities and incorporating twenty-first-century tools such as video and social media, I was able to build the students' capacity for working in teams and subsequently brought my project design into better alignment with what students can expect to encounter in today's workforce. Students were inspired and took the time to let me know. They reported improvement in specific communication skills as well as a command of techniques and strategies for working in groups and teams. I received comments like these:

"We continued to work on our listening skills by actively involving every member in our team discussions. We all asked questions about the others' statements and took time to listen carefully to what was said, ask questions, and restate what was heard. These techniques were especially helpful in developing our Project Plan."

"As a whole I really liked this project because it forced us into an uncomfortable environment and made us work together for a common goal.

The project built a lot of confidence in communicating with others and being able to get your point across."

Students felt empowered by their new mastery of the "real world" social media tools they used to manage the project, and there was evidence that they felt the experience was worthwhile:

"Before this assignment and before this class in general I had no idea what GoogleDocs was or that you could video conference and share documents instantly like that. It's really quite amazing that you can share documents with someone across the world."

"It's something we will take away from this class and use in real life; I'm going to start using it at work!"

"I will bring many positive things away from this project. I now have the knowledge of many different online communication tools. Skype, Twitter, and GoogleDocs were all very useful and I will continue to use them."

As organizations rely more and more on the virtual team structure, it is imperative that we give students meaningful opportunities to work collaboratively and practice the communications skills they will need to succeed beyond the classroom.

References

Carr, Deacon, et al. 2005. *The team learning assistant workbook.* New York: McGraw-Hill.

McTighe and Wiggins. 1998. *Understanding by Design.* Alexandria, VA: The Association for Supervision and Curriculum Development.

PMI Educational Foundation. 2006. PM skills for life manual. *Project Management Institute Educational Foundation.* www.pmi.org/pmief.

Reprinted from *Online Classroom*, June 2011.

Alternative Assessment Methods for the Online Classroom

by Rob Kelly

Tests and quizzes are often the primary means of assessing online learner performance; however, as Rena Palloff and Keith Pratt, online instructors and coauthors of numerous online learning books, including *Lessons from the Virtual Classroom: The Realities of Online Teaching* (2013), point out, there are more effective and less problematic alternatives.

They cite three significant drawbacks of test and quizzes:

- Test and quizzes typically assess low-level learning. "They address only some of the lower levels of Bloom's Taxonomy, often sticking to the knowledge level. [Tests and quizzes] measure how much information students have memorized and then can spit back out on an exam. Most test questions are not designed to allow students to engage in really critical thinking or analysis or synthesis of materials," Palloff says.

- Tests and quizzes often are not aligned with the learning objectives or pedagogies of the course. "When you're having students do more authentic activities or application activities, you're working at the higher levels of Bloom's Taxonomy—synthesis or evaluation—but then you're measuring the lowest level—the knowledge level—by using a test or quiz," Palloff and Pratt say.

- This misalignment issue arose in an online course Palloff and Pratt taught together. The course was primarily discussion based. They had students do things such as discuss news articles that illustrated concepts in the course. "The discussion activities were really robust, very practical, very applied, and authentic. And then they were given a final exam out of the blue that we did not write, and all the students failed. It was a picky final exam with true-false and multiple-choice questions. Every student failed because that was not the way the course was taught. They were taught to think at much higher levels, and they went into this final exam that was all about rote memorization of stuff from the textbook . . . It wasn't a good way to measure how they were actually doing in the course," Palloff and Pratt say.

- Overuse of test and quizzes can promote cheating. Several studies have shown that when tests and quizzes are the primary means of assessment, students cheat more than they would if they engaged in a more authentic activity, Palloff says.

Authentic, learner-centered, collaborative assessment alternatives

Alternative assessment methods such as writing assignments, collaborative assignments, case studies, and debates can avoid the problems often associated with tests and quizzes. "There are many ways to approach assessment. It depends on the context of the course. When we teach faculty how to teach online, we try to give them a taste of a majority of those methods. I don't know that we can cover all of them in one course, but there are multiple ways to get at the issues and make this a real-life situation for the students so they can actually learn from the process," Pratt says.

Palloff and Pratt recommend selecting assessment methods that are learner-centered and authentic.

Learner-centered assessment methods address whether the learner has met the learning outcomes of the course as well as how the learner got there. "A learner-centered assessment is an assessment that links what the student is learning in the course to the assessment process," Palloff says.

Authentic assessment methods can reduce cheating. One way to make assignments more authentic and less susceptible to cheating is to have students embed their own experiences in their assignments. "For example, if they are writing about human development, you can have them write about their own development. They're writing about themselves, and that is very difficult to buy through a paper mill or to plagiarize," Palloff says.

Mobile technology is one way to incorporate authentic assessment into a course. For example, one of Pratt's doctoral students uses mobile phones in a 12th-grade calculus course he teaches. Students record themselves working on problems. "This allows them to move around. They can get creative. It challenges them to do a multitude of things on different levels and they're learning calculus in the process," Pratt says.

Palloff also uses mobile technology for authentic assignments. As part of a final project in a community health care course, she has students prepare a brief proposal to their communities about the development of a particular health service. Students then go out and interview community members and record the interviews using cell phones. "There are lots of ways to use the technologies that are available to us to enhance those kinds of products. Students can then post those online so that other students can see them and give them feedback in addition to the instructor's evaluation," Palloff says.

When students do collaborative assignments, they should be assessed collaboratively, Palloff and Pratt say. Collaborative assessment is a combination of students assessing themselves and one another and the instructor taking that input and doing the final assessment. In addition to providing a basis for a grade, these collaborative assessments provide useful insights on what worked and what didn't work on an assignment, which Palloff and Pratt debrief with students so that they can reflect on what they might do differently the next time.

Appropriate uses of tests and quizzesWhen used sparingly and properly designed, tests and quizzes can be useful assessment methods, Palloff and Pratt say.

Rather than relying on anti-cheating technologies or proctors, they recommend using open-book tests and quizzes "because students are going to have their text material available, and if they are working online they can look things up on Google," Palloff says. "There are all kinds of ways that they can gather information, and, the truth is, in the real world if the student comes up against a problem or an issue that they don't have the answer to, they're going to look it up or ask someone. So if you construct your tests and quizzes that way you're actually teaching students some skills that they're going to use when they get out of school."

The questions in an open-book test or quiz need to be complex and require students to know the material and know where to look if they are uncertain about something. When open-book tests or quizzes are well designed, students who don't do the work will not be able to do well on them even with an open book.

Reprinted from *Online Classroom*, July 2013.

Effective Feedback Strategies for the Online Classroom

by Jean Mandernach and Jennifer Garrett

Feedback is more than post-assignment commentary. When employed correctly, feedback can impact students on a variety of levels. It helps direct what they should do with their time, how they should feel about their efforts, whether their motivation level is appropriate, whether they are meeting expectations, and more.

Because feedback serves so many purposes in the online classroom, it is important for instructors to consider how feedback is provided, when it is offered, how it is focused or targeted, and what is considered in the feedback.

Best practices consider feedback holistically and address three key elements: timing, target, and nature. It is important for instructors to be deliberate about all three factors and use care when determining when to deliver feedback, what the feedback should say, and what the feedback is meant to accomplish.

First, feedback must be timely if it is to be effective. This means it is consistent, immediate, ongoing, incremental, and formative. Feedback must also be targeted. It should be communicated directly to the learner and specific to the task at hand. Feedback should address effort and whether the student appropriately processed the task. Targeted feedback, however, does not have to be direct communication between the instructor and one student. It can be peer-based, individual, or group.

Finally, instructors need to consider the nature of their feedback. It should be corrective and specifically identify where, if at all, students veered off course. It should be concrete and specific so students understand which portion of the task they completed incorrectly or which course material they failed to understand. Feedback should reference assignment criteria so that it appears founded and appropriate. It should be useful and actionable; instructors should give suggestions on how to redress problems and make improvements in the next assignments. It isn't enough to tell students that they did something wrong; instructors need to explain how to do it better the next time. Tone is also very important, particularly without in-person rapport to modulate criticism. To this point, instructors need to take care to compliment what students do well and to sandwich criticism in more positive feedback.

When delivered effectively, feedback is a tool that develops cognitive understanding, motivation and engagement, and interpersonal connections. It not only helps students learn course material but also helps keep them motivated, engaged in what can feel like an isolated environment, and connected to the course. Feedback can foster interpersonal connections between instructors and students. It can even foster connections among students. All told, feedback has a direct bearing on whether students have meaningful interactions with course materials and overall positive course experiences. Because feedback can be such a powerful tool, it behooves instructors to endeavor to get the most impact from the feedback they provide.

The Challenge of Online Teaching

As is the case with many aspects of instruction, the issue with feedback is not that instructors don't know what they should be doing. Rather, it is that instructors don't have the time to provide the kind of feedback they would like to deliver. With one teacher and 10, 15, 20, or even 50 students per course (and often multiple courses taught per term), it can be daunting and even impossible to fulfill feedback best practices. In any given week, instructors face an exponential buildup of student artifacts that demand time and attention. It is an overwhelming challenge to maintain a desirable level and quality of feedback without overinvesting, which can lead to instructor burnout.

It is important to note that the goal is not to improve feedback by spending more time on it. Rather, the goal is to optimize time spent on feedback so that instructors can invest an appropriate amount of effort and get high-quality results. It's the adage of working smarter, not harder.

There are tools and strategies that will allow instructors to shift the balance and invest their time in a manner and place that yield high-quality feedback that impacts student learning while still leaving time for other high-impact activities. After all, feedback is important, but it isn't the only activity that matters.

Instructional Strategies

Effective and efficient feedback comes down to three broad strategies.

The first is time management. Instructors who struggle with feedback may need to consider how they manage their time. They should look at not only how much time they spend on each course but also whether they are spending the most time on the activities with the highest impact and the least time on the activities with the lowest impact.

The second strategy is to embrace emergent technologies. Technology can automate some repetitive feedback tasks to improve efficiency without diminishing quality.

The third strategy is to adopt a more holistic feedback approach that views feedback as a more organic element of instruction and not something that is delivered only after an assignment is submitted.

Time Management

Providing feedback is just one facet of online instruction. An instructor is responsible for myriad tasks and must meet a variety of obligations. Prioritizing efforts and allocating an appropriate amount of time to all instructional practices is a constant balancing act for most instructors, but there are some principles to guide them.

On a broad level, the role of the instructor can be broken down into three categories of activities: teaching, grading and feedback, and administration.

Teaching

For years adult-learning theory has said that online courses are filled with adult learners and that instructors are there to facilitate adult learners. However, that is a limited view of the role of the online instructor. While the "sage on the stage" model is outdated and ill-suited to online education, instructors are still subject matter experts who are teaching because they have knowledge, both in terms of breadth and mastery that their students do not have.

Instructors are valued, at least in part, for the degrees they have earned and for the scholarship they produce. This expertise and knowledge are valuable not only to institutions but also to students, and both should be tapped for students' benefits. Instructors certainly are facilitators now more than at any other time, but they still have a responsibility to share and bestow information. Classroom activities should utilize this expertise to impact student learning.

Grading and feedback

No one argues that grading and feedback are not important. Research overwhelmingly shows that students pay attention and respond to grades. They guide their time, their attention, and their effort based on the grades they are getting. Thus, grading and feedback can be effective tools for focusing students' attention. For this to work, however, grading must be aligned with learning objectives, and feedback must move students toward those learning objectives. Also imperative is that grading and feedback are consistent and timely. All the pieces must work together to have the most impact.

Administration

Course administration or management is also a necessary component of instruction. Course management might include answering how-to questions, guiding students through the learning management system, or helping troubleshoot technical issues. This is particularly important for online students who will struggle if they cannot navigate course technology. Technology should create learning opportunities, not barriers. Overall, instructors need to keep courses well organized and functional so that small issues or annoyances do not interfere with learning.

Reprinted from the whitepaper *Efficient and Effective Feedback in the Online Classroom.*

Selecting Feedback Techniques

by Rob Kelly

There are many ways to provide feedback to students in an online course. When selecting the type and frequency of feedback, consider what the students want and how they will benefit from it without creating an unreasonable amount of work for yourself. In an interview with *Online Classroom*, Rosemary Cleveland, professor of education, and Kim Kenward, instructional designer at Grand Valley State University, offered the following advice on how to manage feedback in the online learning environment:

Be timely with feedback

"If you don't start off at the beginning giving them feedback that has meaning for them, the quality of their work slips. If you give them good, strong feedback at the beginning that's very personal, constructive, and helpful, the quality of their work [will be better] for the whole semester. If they know that somebody really cares about what they're doing and [makes] that personal connection, they will work to that expectation. If they don't think the instructor is spending time with their work and simply says, 'Oh, you did a great job' but doesn't make anything personal, they figure, 'Oh well, the instructor skimmed the information,'" Cleveland said.

Start with a positive message

Thank the student and say something positive about his or her work before discussing areas that need to be improved. A positive message provides encouragement and makes students feel "that they really are part of the learning community ... and that the class can take on personal meaning for them," Cleveland said.

In addition, Cleveland said that it's important to include examples from students' work so they know that you have read it.

Scaffold assignments

Assigning tasks that are relatively easy in the beginning and get progressively difficult provides students with opportunities for success, which builds confidence.

Help students see the connection between the course and their lives

One way to do this is to use the private journal feature found in many learning management systems. "It's a good complement to the discussion board," Cleveland said. "It allows students to make personal connections in their own lives in terms of what they're reading about in the course . . . The private journal is that almost one-on-one communication between the online student and the instructor."

Use rubrics

Rubrics provide criteria for students to see how their work compares with expectations and helps them focus their work. Students can help create rubrics.

Consider various formats

Most instructors (and students) are comfortable with feedback provided in text formats—whether it's through the track changes function of Word, an email message, or measuring an assignment against a detailed rubric—but there are other options. Audio feedback can provide opportunities for nuanced feedback. It also can create a sense of instructor presence and a personal connection between student and instructor.

In a survey of their students, approximately 70 percent liked having audio feedback because they could hear the instructor's voice, which makes the message more personal, "almost like a conversation," Cleveland said.

"Overall, we're seeing a trend at our university for more oral feedback. Our students are craving it. They're asking their instructors to use the Grade Center [within Blackboard] to provide more detailed feedback," Kenward said.

Audio feedback offers benefits to instructors as well. For example, a student teacher who used audio feedback said, "Voice feedback reduces the amount of time that it takes to respond to the students [because] most faculty, like myself, can talk faster than they can type."

Here's another student comment: "I think that adding a voice file to my graded comments was worthwhile. It adds a personal feel to the online course, and it's good to receive audio feedback, which contains many elements that are lacking in written feedback."

One way to embed video is by using software such as Audacity to create MP3 files. Some versions of Blackboard feature a tool called Voice Collaborate that enables users to embed audio, Slideshare, YouTube, or Flickr anywhere within the LMS by clicking on the mashup plugin that appears in every part of Blackboard. (Students also have the ability to use this feature.)

Find a system that works for you

Providing frequent feedback can create a workload issue. This is why it's important to find ways of doing it that make it as easy as possible. Cleveland, for example, takes notes as she reads students' assignments. "If I can have three or four phrases based on what the students said and then respond to it, it's much easier for me—I don't have to respond to everything they say, but if I can respond to two or three key points in the journal or discussion board, they know that it's a meaningful response," she said.

Kenward said that some instructors use dual monitors—one to view each student's assignment and one to access a spreadsheet to enter feedback.

Provide opportunities for peer feedback

On a major assignment in one of her courses, Cleveland requires students to provide feedback to each other before submitting the assignment for a grade. Students submit their work to the discussion board, and a partner offers feedback using a detailed rubric Cleveland provides. Each student can then make improvements before submitting it for a grade. In addition, this provides a way for students to engage with each other. "We thought that was a positive addition to the [course]," Cleveland said.

Reprinted from *Online Classroom*, January 2013.

Assessing Learning through Student Screencasts

by John Orlando, Northcentral University

Technology has transformed how education is delivered. Yet the digital revolution has not had a dramatic influence on how students are assessed. Most instructors are still using the standard exams, problem sets, or papers to assess student learning.

The problem with these methods is that they show only the product; they do not demonstrate the process that was used to develop the product, and process is everything. Normally, a failure in product is produced by a failure in process. Was the work disorganized? Then the student does not know how to organize an assignment. Did the student misrepresent an idea from a reading? Then the student might not know how to read academic work.

The thinking that went into developing a work is probably the most important information that an instructor needs to help a student with performance problems. Illuminating that thinking is sometimes called "making thinking visible." This can be harder to do in an online course, where the instructor does not have the face-to-face moments with students.

But technology now allows instructors to view students' thinking online using screencasts—a simple video recording of what happens on the monitor, with voice narration. Students can use screencasts to describe the process that went into developing their work, thus cluing in their instructors to problems with process.

David Woods, assistant professor of computer and information technology at Miami University, uses student screencasts in his computer programming classes. Students write code to execute a particular program and hand it in for their assignment. But they also make screencasts that answer various questions about their thinking in writing the code.

On the first assignment, they were required to make an observation about the C++ computer language that they used to make the code, since it was new to them. They could talk about how the language differs from those that they had previously worked with. They could also talk about parts of the language that they did not understand. This exercise forced the students to reflect on the course material and their struggles with it, and allowed the instructor to ascertain the student's true level of understanding.

On the next assignment, students were required to make a screencast that showed the code executing, as well as discuss their experience writing the code. For instance, they could discuss the hardest section for them to write.

One nice outcome of the screencasts was that Dr. Woods was able to come up with questions for students to answer on future screencasts based on what he saw from past screencasts. If a student had a particular problem, Dr. Woods could ask the student to talk on the next screencast about how he or she addressed it. This ensured that the students were thinking about their performance and Dr. Woods' feedback on it. Dr. Woods might also ask students whether they considered alternate ways to code some parts of the program. Thus, the system allowed customized assessment and student reflection.

Dr. Woods also used screencasts to move students beyond merely developing the program. Once they had become familiar with writing in the new language, they were asked to make a screencast that trained others to write code for a particular function. This forced them to consider not only how they write code, but also how they could explain the process in a way that someone else could understand. The result is a deeper understanding of the material.

Finally, students were given the option at the end of class of presenting their work to others in a screencast. This gave them the experience of presenting their work to others as they would do in a face-to-face class or conference but doing it in an online environment.

Dr. Woods discovered a number of unexpected benefits of the screencast system. First, it made grading easier because the screencasts provided information that was not obvious from the code itself. Much of grading involves making inferences about the student's level of understanding of the assignment, and the screencasts can fill in the missing information.

Second, the screencasts provided fodder for discussion questions. Most online courses have all discussion questions set up at the beginning of the course. But the screencasts gave Dr. Woods ideas for new or alternate questions to ask. In particular, he could ask the class questions related to areas in which the students reported struggles in their screencasts. The screencasts thus served as a formative assessment that allowed the instructor to make adjustments to the course format on the fly.

Third, students treated the screencasts as a conversation with the instructor. While students usually view assignments as just a means of checking off a class requirement, the students genuinely communicated their thoughts and concerns to their instructor through the screencasts. The assignments became more than just attempts to impress for a grade. They became an opportunity for a meeting of the minds on course concepts.

Fourth, the screencasts led students to reevaluate and correct their work. This might be due to students' taking more ownership of the work when they had to present it in a screencast. It seemed also due to students' identifying issues with their work as they talked about it during the screencast. Some students would even pause the recording to fix an issue that cropped up during the screencast. It is well known that students do not review their work enough before handing it in, and the screencasts forced this review and subsequent improvements in performance.

Finally, students were proud enough of their screencasts that many shared them with friends and family. How often do students share regular assignments with others? This demonstrates how we tend to want to share our digital artifacts with others.

Interestingly, none of the students had any questions about how to make a screencast. Dr. Woods suggested Screencast-o-matic as an option, which allows users to create screencasts that are easily uploaded to the Screencast-o-matic website. Students can then simply send the instructor a link to the screen to view. Jing is another option that allows for screencasts up to five minutes long. But Dr. Woods found that many students loaded the videos to YouTube. Some used the free Google Hangouts on Air feature in Google+ to record their screencasts, which automatically uploads the result to their YouTube account.

Dr. Woods also noted that some students submitted the actual video files through the LMS. However, these files can be quite large, and one was too large for the LMS to handle. Plus, the process can require long uploading and downloading times on the parts of student and instructor.

Screencasting assignments should work in nearly any field. Engineering students could describe their thinking in designing models, while students working on math or physics problems could be asked to describe how they analyzed and solved problems in an assignment.

Consider incorporating screencasting assignments into your online courses.

Reference

Woods, D. 2015. Student-created screencasts as an aid to grading and tool for student reflection. EdMedia conference, Montreal.

Reprinted from *Online Classroom*, September 2015.

Quality Feedback in Less Time Online

by Jean Mandernach, Grand Canyon University

I *know* the importance of providing feedback on students' written work. There is a plethora of research on the value of feedback for impacting student learning, motivation, and engagement in the online classroom. There are just as many empirically driven "best practices" to guide faculty inclusion of feedback. But *knowing* what I should do and actually *doing* it are two separate issues.

Despite the ever-growing body of evidence that unequivocally supports the need for clear, detailed, timely feedback in response to students' work, the practical demands of the online classroom leave me struggling to translate pedagogical knowledge into practice. Let's face it: There is a lot of written work in an online classroom. From threaded discussions to homework assignments to formal papers, the text-driven nature of the asynchronous learning environment produces a mountain of student artifacts that demand my individualized attention. At any given time, I may have 20– 40 students (depending on the number of courses I am teaching), and there is, invariably, only one of me. As such, the challenge is not in knowing how to provide effective feedback; it is in finding the time to do it.

My quest for instructional efficiency has led to the development of a number of realistic, practical strategies for providing high-quality, individualized feedback in less time. Underlying these strategies is the ability to streamline repetitive feedback tasks. Like most faculty, I find my students make a relatively consistent range of errors (whether in relation to general writing strategies, citation style, or conceptual misunderstandings). Rather than invest my time in responding individually to these issues, I can regain time through the repurposing of common feedback comments, incorporation of one-to-many feedback approaches, and integration of "feedforward" strategies.

For example, one of the common challenges for students learning to write in the social sciences is mastering APA style. While the writing and citation style may or may not be the focus of the assignment, best practices dictate that I should provide feedback on students' writing in addition to the conceptual objectives integral to the assignment. The first few times I come across APA style errors, I find it relatively easy and painless to utilize the comment feature of Microsoft Word to provide elaborative, detailed feedback that not only highlights the errors but also provides a correct example and directs students toward appropriate resources. By the nineteenth time I come across these same APA style errors, not only has my feedback been reduced to a cursory (and not remotely helpful) "improper APA style" comment, but I also have invested considerable time in the feedback process without having an equivalent return in potential student learning.

Repurposing feedback

Through the repurposing of feedback, I can save these types of common feedback comments to reuse when appropriate on other student work. The efficiency value of repurposing feedback lies not only in the ability to quickly and easily insert these saved feedback comments into students' work but also in the investment of time required to create the initial feedback comment. Because the feedback statement is likely to be used repeatedly, it justifies the additional time investment required to create elaborative feedback that includes examples, links to additional resources, and other relevant information.

While on a basic level repurposed feedback could simply be saved and copied/pasted into a document as appropriate, there are a number of programs (i.e., PhraseExpress, TypeItIn, Presto, etc.) that automate this process and allow for the insertion of saved custom feedback comments in response to programmed hot keys. Similarly, I simply utilize the autocorrect feature of Microsoft Word to create a custom feedback library that can insert saved comments into Word documents to replace preprogrammed text as I type. The result is the ability to provide extensive, elaborative feedback across an entire class of student papers in a minimal amount of time, without sacrificing quality.

One-to-many feedback

In addition to creating my own custom feedback library, I also maintain a list of the most common conceptual, technical, and mechanical strengths and errors that emerge from the students' work on a particular assignment. At the completion of all individual grading, I create a reflective overview of generalized feedback in relation to the specific assignment and post this feedback to the entire class. In this manner, I can provide an informal social comparison that allows students to reflect on the strengths and weaknesses of their work in relation to their classmates', and I am able to ensure that all students have access to essential instructional resources. To maximize efficiency from semester to semester, I maintain this document as a "living resource" that continues to change, grow, and adapt in relation to the students' work and available outside resources.

Feedforward strategies

Beyond providing summative feedback to correct errors that have already occurred in submitted assignments, I monitor the themes that emerge as challenge areas to create feedforward resources to minimize errors from happening in the first place. As described by Goldsmith (2002), rather than focusing on past mistakes, feedforward information provides individuals with resources, strategies, and ideas to help them be successful before they begin a task. As such, prior to each assignment, I post a feedforward announcement that provides extra information, guidance, and resource links to help students avoid common errors and to produce higher-quality artifacts. The result is student assignments that simply require less individualized, corrective feedback and, therefore, less time to grade.

Conclusion

Detailed, elaborative feedback is an essential component of effective learning in the online classroom. The inclusion of efficient feedback strategies helps bridge the gap between knowledge and behavior in relation to online instructional practices. By streamlining the feedback process through the repurposing of feedback, incorporation of one-to-many approaches, and integration of feedforward strategies, I am able to provide high-quality feedback in an efficient manner that frees instructional time to be invested in other aspects of teaching.

Reference

Goldsmith, M. 2002. Try feedforward instead of feedback. *Leader to Leader*. Retrieved from marshallgoldsmithlibrary.com/cim/articles_display.php?aid=110.

Reprinted from *Online Classroom*, June 2013.

Online Learning 2.0: Screencasting Feedback

by John Orlando, Northcentral University

Research has shown that voice feedback:

- Increases student retention of both the feedback itself, and the content to which the feedback refers
- Facilitates a sense of greater instructor caring
- Allows for more feedback in less time
- • Improves a student's ability to understand nuance
Reduces a student's sense of isolation

But instructors can do one better by delivering feedback through screencasting. A screencast is a recording of the action on a monitor along with voice narration. Many people already use it to record tutorials on technical functions, such as how to post a discussion message to an online forum. Screencasts are easy to make. You simply open the software, define the area to be recorded by dragging your cursor across the monitor to make a rectangular field, click "record," and start speaking and doing. The system will record everything that happens on the monitor along with the narration.

Screencasting is an ideal way for instructors to add a visual component to voice feedback, and make the experience similar to the student sitting next to them in the office. The instructor records his or her comments while highlighting passages in the student's work where the feedback applies. A faculty member can say "Here you talked about this particular concept, but notice that you did not include a discussion of this related concept. It should have gone right here." Now students get both the voice comments and an understanding of where they apply.

For instance, very often a student's problem is in the organization of their work. Paragraphs might be in the wrong place, or ideas fragmented and spread across a paper. A screencast allows the instructor to not only highlight the problems, but also move the passages around the work in front of the student's eyes so that the student can see alternate organizations. Now the student gets the benefit of not only learning the problem, but seeing the solution. Screencasting has the additional benefit that is it recorded, so the student can go back over it again piece by piece later to recall points, unlike a live session where the points can be forgotten or misremembered later.

Systems

Jing

One of the simplest screencasting tools is Jing, made by Techsmith. Jing allows for recordings up to five minutes long. Once done, the result can be saved on the user's desktop as a video file, or uploaded to Screencast. com, Techsmith's free cloud-based video hosting system. Cloud hosting is the preferable method, since video files can be quite large—often too large for an email attachment or to be sent through an LMS's messaging system. Once the video is loaded to the cloud, the instructor merely has to provide students with a link to the video and they can play it on their own.

Screencast-O-Matic

Screencast-O-Matic has the advantage of allowing for screencasts up to 15 minutes long that can be uploaded to the cloud. Unlike Jing, the free version produces a watermark over the video, but the paid version is only $15 per year, and well worth the investment. Plus, Screencast-O-Matic allows you to record yourself by webcam at the same time that you record the screen, with the webcam shot showing up as a smaller box in the corner of the video. This is a potentially valuable addition, because much of communication comes through non-verbal cues such as facial expressions. The student will be more focused on the feedback when they can see the instructor's face. Even the mere presence of a face helps remind the student that the instructor is a person, which improves the sense of social presence, and can help comfort a student if the feedback points out particularly severe deficiencies.

Camtasia Studio

Camtasia Studio is Techsmith's paid screencasting and editing software, and something to strongly consider if you plan to get serious about screencasting. Camtasia Studio is also an excellent video editing tool, and ideal for putting together video content for an online course. Techsmith just released Camtasia Relay, which comes free with Camtasia Studio, and allows you to record your webcam with your screencast, just like Screencast-O-Matic. One nice feature is the ability to change the size of the webcam shot in the video. You might want to start a video with just a shot of your face through the webcam, then shrink that when you are directing the viewer's attention to the monitor, and enlarge it again for your conclusion. This can create a great effect for feedback or a tutorial.

Reprinted from *Online Classroom*, April 2014.

Use Collaborative Assessments for Collaborative Work

by Rob Kelly

If you use collaborative assignments in your online course, you should assess those assignments collaboratively, said Rena Palloff, online instructor and coauthor (with Keith Pratt) of several online learning books, including *Lessons from the Virtual Classroom: The Realities of Online Teaching* (2013).

"We're firm believers that if you're going to give a collaborative activity, you should assess it collaboratively. And what that means is that we ask students to tell us how they think they did as well as how they think their peers did in that collaborative activity. Obviously, those are privately shared communications, although we do debrief with the group in terms of how they thought the process went.

"And the information that's gathered from those private communications really shouldn't be given less emphasis than what you observe or evaluate less directly as the instructor, because oftentimes students will tell us in private communications things we don't see, things that might have happened off-line.

"Group members assess themselves and their peers. They evaluate the process. Always, the veto power remains with us as instructors, and there have been times I've had to use that veto. But for the most part, the collaborative assessment happens within the group.

"We generally recommend using both group and individual grades. And so the students get an individual grade for their participation, and then the group gets a grade for the product they produced."

Reprinted from *Online Classroom*, November 2013.

Online Feedback: Google Drive Is Your Best Friend

by John Orlando, Northcentral University

Some technologies become so ubiquitous that we wonder how we ever got along without them. How did people cook before microwaves, and how did we get money out of banks before ATMs?

Google Drive is one of those technologies. Drive is Google's cloud-based suite of collaboration apps that has fundamentally changed how we work together, and once you start using it, you will wonder how you ever got along without it. Even those who use Drive are generally unaware of the full scope of its functionality and potential. Below are some uses for Drive that will transform how you teach and grade.

Shared document editing

In the past, when we worked together on documents by sending them around as email attachments, the result was multiple versions floating around, with edits being made to old versions and time lost trying to blend different versions. For this reason, all my work group's collaboration is now done with Google Docs, a Drive app. We put the document in a shared folder on Docs, meaning that all edits are made to the exact same document, and everyone knows where to go to get the latest version.

This collaboration can also apply to student work. Have your students do both individual and group work with a document created using Google Docs that they share with you. That way you can monitor their progress to make sure that they are moving along. You can also have students in group projects color-code their contributions so you can see who is contributing or not contributing. This makes the development process itself visual to you, whereas the development process was formerly mysterious to us. Now you can see problems as they arise and head them off.

What's more, there is no reason to download the student's work at the end in order to grade it. Just add your feedback to the Google Docs version itself. The work and feedback are preserved in a place that both instructor and student can return to at any time for questions or discussion. Plus, there are no more "the email must have lost it" excuses for missing work.

Another good use of Google Docs is to provide students with a template that scaffolds their thinking. We frequently give students assignments that are too open-ended and then penalize them for going off in the wrong direction. Students often need to have their thinking tracked with some simple parameters. You can do this by creating a template document with section headings or some similar scaffolding that students download and then fill in. Since it is on Drive, they simply copy that template into their own folders, rename it, and fill it in, and when it's done you can take a look at it—all without sending documents back and forth. Now students have an easy way to access the scaffolding and no way to "lose" their work, while you have an easy way to view the result and even monitor its development.

There are a few newer features of Google Docs that now make this tool even more powerful for teaching. First, the new commenting feature allows collaborators to add content to a document in three different ways. First, they can edit the document directly. Second, they can suggest edits in a track-changes-style format. Students might want to use this function when they are suggesting edits to someone else's contributions. That way the student can spend some time reflecting on the suggested change rather than just having the change just show up, which makes the process a learning opportunity. Finally, someone can post a comment similar to a margin comment in Word, which you as the instructor can use to ask questions of the group or to suggest different directions for their work. Students can even reply directly to the comment itself.

Document hosting

You can also use Drive as a general site for hosting content, including documents, presentations, and videos, that you want to share with others. Essentially, you are using Drive as your personal website without having to learn website development. Create a shared folder for each of your classes with all the documents in it. Share it with them once and they will immediately have access to anything you add to it. No more sending around content.

Shared folders are also very handy for professional presentations or workshops, as they provide an easy way of getting electronic material to audience members. When I give a presentation or workshop, I create a Drive folder that includes all the content of the presentation as well as additional resources, videos, tutorials, etc. Then I make a one-page handout that includes links to that folder and a QR code to it so that everyone can reach the material with a snap of their cell phones or tablets. Now I can have workshop attendees download anything that I want them to work on or to keep as a reference right from that handout, and I don't bother printing 50 workbooks of 20 pages each anymore.

In addition, goo.gl can be used to create shortened URLs, much like bitly does. But it also creates a QR code with the URL for you to download. Just click "details" in the results to find it.

Forms

Google Forms is a very powerful Drive function that is rapidly gaining a loyal audience among teachers. Essentially, Forms allows you to make an online form to collect information such as survey or quiz responses. You might want to survey your students at the beginning of your class on topics such as their educational background or expectations of the class as well as their preferred contact methods. The results are automatically collected in a spreadsheet created within Drive.

But Forms can also be a powerful way of delivering instruction itself. Traditional online courses separate the content delivery from reflection. Students watch a video or read an article in one place and then discuss it later in a separate discussion forum. Now there is a "distance" between engagement with the content and reflection, and students often forget any questions that they might have had and generally lose much of what they saw.

Google Forms can be used to deliver teaching models that integrate content with reflection. For instance, imagine that you are teaching a module on ethical issues in genetic testing. You can build the module as a Google Form by embedding videos, links to websites or documents, and all the content you like. Importantly, each piece of content is immediately followed by a question for reflection. The question could be a simple multiple-choice or short-answer response to ensure that students watched and understood the content. It could also require a short discussion of the student's thoughts or questions.

I teach an online class for faculty on the role of relationships in teaching. I use Google Forms to deliver the module by alternating short videos about the topic with examples of faculty interaction with students. Each video and example is followed by a question that forces the faculty member to discuss the content, and even suggest alternate ways to convey the message that was given in the examples. Now participants are applying what they learn as they learn it, and they're stopping to reflect on content before it is forgotten.

Spreadsheets

Google Spreadsheets is a powerful alternative to an Excel file. My team manages the training for about 400 faculty and so it needs a common source to track faculty status between and within each training. Using Google Spreadsheets was by far the easiest option. The entire training problem is captured as columns in the spreadsheet, along with important correspondence and any issues. Now everyone on my team knows exactly where to go to get up-to-date information on any faculty member's status.

One advantage of Google Spreadsheets is that the [Control]+[F] function allows users to quickly find any information they want. This is a feature of all browsers and will take you to all instances within a Web page where the search term is found. Finding a particular faculty member takes literally a few moments.

You might consider using Google Spreadsheets to host student information. The spreadsheet can track assignment completion, which makes it easy to find those who are falling behind. It can also host your thoughts on student work in order to track their progress throughout the class. Finally, you can include agreements made with students, such as extensions, in order keep track of your promises and see when students are making repeated requests.

There are a myriad of ways that Google Drive will improve your teaching and grading work. Start using these systems and you will wonder how you ever lived without them.

Reprinted from *Online Classroom*, December 2014.

Using Student Analytics for Online Course Improvement

by Jennifer Patterson Lorenzetti, managing editor Academic Leader

Many instructors feel that they need to be experts in mathematics in order to understand analytics. But according to John Vivolo, director of online and virtual learning for New York University, every faculty member can learn to use the course analytics available through their LMS to improve student learning.

Vivolo's aim is to help faculty "use analytics to proactively reach out to students." Vivolo talks about what he calls "pocket data analytics." These are small, easy-to-use pieces of data that are readily available to instructors through their LMS.

Pocket data analytics are a way to leverage the data that is collected, often automatically, by looking at smaller bits of data that show discrete happenings and student behaviors in a class. This allows instructors, deans, and instructional designers to move beyond simple surveys and student grades as metrics into more information that is easily understood and responded to.

In a paper for the International Conference on Analytics Driven Solutions in 2014, Vivolo explains the concept this way: "Rather than looking at large scale data, the purpose of this method is to get instructors to focus on smaller patterns within a single course, during a specific time period, such as a week. The intent is to have a method in which to introduce the concept of academic course analytics as a practical tool."

Vivolo highlights three types of analytics that are readily-available and easily used:

Time-based

Time-based measures are probably the type of analytic that faculty members are most familiar with. For example, data may show that students log into the class more often on weekends or more often late at night or at lunchtime. The faculty member may then find ways to tailor her own schedule to the needs of the students and the goals of the course.

For instance, a faculty member may decide that it would be best to encourage students to log in at times other than the weekend, and so she may decide to release assignments and discussion board comments mid-week. Or a faculty member may realize that her class is made up of many working professionals and may elect to give the majority of the information on the weekends when more students are logging in.

In a paper on the subject, Vivolo says, "When looking at these numbers, an instructor should consider the demographics of their students. One cannot ignore the variety of student populations when comparing online to on-campus learning. Are they working students who have less time to access the course during the week and must access it during the weekends? Are they more traditional students who can access material during the day (assuming they do not have a full-time job)? Are they international [students], national students, or local students?"

Individual assignments/content

Another helpful pocket analytic is the individual item or assignment analytic, such as how often students view a particular course element, such as a video. For example, a single student may view a video many more times compared to the rest of the class. This may indicate that the instructor should intervene in some way, perhaps by asking if there are any questions about the content.

It's important, however, that instructors not use the pocket analytics in a way that makes students feel uncomfortable. In the above example, asking the individual student why he or she viewed the video so many times would probably be inappropriate. "I won't recommend doing things with a Big Brother mentality," Vivolo says. Instead, data points like this might cue the instructor to send a general invitation for any student with questions so that the answer may be discussed. Additionally, data that suggests that more than one student is viewing a particular piece of course information repeatedly may be an indication that the information is difficult or unclear. In this case, the faculty member "can host a review or re-record the lecture," Vivolo says. He also advises that instructors refrain from moving on in a course until they are convinced their students understand the material.

Discussion boards

Discussion boards are another common tool that generates usable data. "Discussion board forums are the most commonly used interactive tool and have been around since online learning started. Its purpose is usually to simulate an in-class discussion, but in an asynchronous method. But how do instructors impress upon students the importance of contributing to the discussion without forcing them to participate?" Vivolo asks.

Once again, data such as log-in times and frequencies are readily available to the instructor. The challenge is in how to use such data. One way is to use log-in and posting data to keep track of attendance. Vivolo cautions against this practice. He quotes an academic article that suggests that activity is not a proxy for monitoring attendance, because students can refrain from posting in a discussion forum and still be reading and thinking about the material.

Vivolo lists techniques to improve discussion board activity, including:
- "Post follow-up questions (randomly) when the replies are the lowest. The students may be more likely to answer follow-up questions from the professor at random times during the week."
- "Create a Discussion Board Interaction Policy, requiring students to post before Wednesday and then another time before another day."
- "Connect [the] discussion board to a major part of the course topics, and thus to a significant part of the student grade."
- "Make the discussion board topics extend over more than one week to allow for additional topics."

Overall, pocket data analytics allow instructors to respond preemptively to student problems and issues before they impact student learning and performance. This is opposed to more reactive approaches in which instructors make course changes only at the end of the course when they see final student results. By using pocket data analytics, instructors can respond in real time to the problems that students have.

Reprinted from *Online Classroom*, March 2015.

Formative Evaluations for Online Education

by Ann Taylor, Penn State, and Jean Mandernach, Grand Canyon University

Traditional measures of teaching effectiveness (i.e., student evaluations, peer review, or administrative evaluation) provide summative feedback that may be useful for enhancing future instructional strategies, but fail to help current students. Instructors need to use formative evaluations to gain feedback about the effectiveness of *current* instructional strategies in order to enhance teaching during the *current* course.

While formative evaluations are useful in all teaching environments, they are particularly beneficial in the online classroom, where gauging teaching effectiveness is more difficult due to the lack of physical presence between student and teacher.

To be most effective, formative evaluations should focus on a specific instructional strategy or concern that is amenable to actionable change. For example, rather than ask a general question, such as, "What aspects of my online teaching have been especially helpful in terms of your learning?" one might ask about a specific teaching strategy that was used, such as, "What do I do in the online discussion forums that helps you understand the course material? How can I interact in the discussions in the future in a manner to help your learning and engagement in the course?" This type of targeted question encourages a richer, deeper response that is more likely to provide insight into how specific instructional strategies can be improved.

For your informal formative evaluations to be effective, they must be intentionally structured and implemented to produce the intended feedback. When developing formative teaching evaluations for use in your online course, consider the five Ws: Who, What, When, Where, and Why:

Who

Unlike summative reviews of teaching that are conducted for administrative purposes, such as promotion or staffing decisions, formative reviews are typically conducted by and for the instructor (perhaps with the support of a learning design team). Given that, you need to determine the relevance, focus, and timing of your formative evaluations.

What

Formative evaluations typically differ from summative reviews of teaching with regard to the type and amount of feedback that is sought. Instructors seeking formative feedback on their teaching typically focus their efforts on specific aspects of their teaching that they would like to improve. For example, instead of an end-of-course student survey that asks about a wide variety of aspects of the course—from questions about the structure of the course to those that address instructor-student interactions—you might ask your students only about a new technique that you recently tried, in order to learn how well the technique was implemented.

When

Because formative evaluations are short, direct measures conducted in response to specific pedagogical questions, formative reviews of teaching are typically conducted more frequently than formal reviews. Although instructors must balance the need for feedback with a respect for students' and peers' time, formative reviews may be conducted at multiple points throughout an online course, from an always-available online "suggestion box" to weekly surveys to mid-semester feedback instruments.

Where

Although summative end-of-course student surveys or administrative reviews are the most common ways to elicit feedback, those take place only at the end of the course and may not be conducted each time the course is taught. Furthermore, they are often conducted outside the course environment. Many instructors have discovered the value of asking for formative feedback much earlier in their courses from directly within the course environment. For example, one might ask students for feedback via in-course strategies such as quick response polls or surveys, discussion forums dedicated to finding out what students think should "start, stop, or continue," or the aforementioned "suggestion box." Likewise, peers might be invited to "visit" the online classroom to review a particular strategy or observe a discussion forum, to help determine how things are going in time to suggest adjustments that will benefit current students.

Why

Instructors should conduct formative evaluations when they are personally interested in improving their teaching and desire feedback in order to do so. Of course, part of their motivation may still be related to ultimate goals of promotion or ensuring that they will continue to be hired to teach a given class in the future, but the primary motivator should be a focus on teaching improvement. By conducting formative reviews of their teaching, instructors are not waiting for periodic summative reviews to get a sense of how they are doing in the online classroom, but are actively soliciting feedback to improve their teaching skills for the benefit of the students currently in their course.

Reprinted from *Online Classroom*, August 2015.

In Praise of Failure

by John Orlando, Northcentral University

One of the biggest failures of higher education is punishing student failure. A bad performance on an assignment is preserved and carried all the way to the final grade. This makes students adverse to risk and obsessed with grades.

But failure is one of our most powerful teaching tools. Many, if not most, of the really important things we learn in life come through failure. I install a kitchen faucet the wrong way, it fails, and from this experience I learn to install it the right way. Learning from failure hardened the lesson in my mind much better than it would have been had I just been told the right way to begin with. As educators, we should be embracing, if not encouraging, student failure as a teaching device.

Coaches understand this principle. NFL coaches will tell rookies not to be afraid of making mistakes in practice because that is the only way they will learn. The worst thing they can do is nothing. Wade Phillips went one step further when he told his team before a preseason game that "your mistakes are my fault; your lack of effort is your fault." Think of the educational view that this comment embodies.

The founders of Google understood the principle. Once during the early years, the Google marketing manager reluctantly informed one of the founders that she had made a mistake that cost the company a million dollars. His response? He told her that he was glad that she made the mistake because it showed that she was taking risks, and the company would never grow without people taking risks. The results speak for themselves. Google is famous for its experimentation, but that experimentation is not possible unless employees know that failure is okay.

Games are powerful learning devices because they allow for low-cost failure. Go through the wrong door and you will get killed and then respawn to try a different door. Failure is not to be feared; it is treated as a learning experience.

We can incorporate failure as a teaching device with assessments that reward final achievement rather than punish mistakes along the way. I worked with a professor who gave everyone in his course an "A" because students were required to revise and resubmit their assignments until they reached "A" work, and then he accepted it. Instead of becoming discouraged by their failures, students knew that they could achieve high grades if they were willing to work and learn from their mistakes.

The online environment is ideal for setting up assessments that reward final achievement. An instructor can have students do multiple-choice quizzes after each reading and allow for resubmissions until the student gets all the questions correct. The instructor can watch the number of submissions to prevent guessing.

We can also use peer assessments to catch student errors before they are submitted. Students can be put into pairs, or small groups, and post their writing assignments to one another to check for clarity, grammar, etc. David Wiley at Brigham Young University had his students post their written work to a blog before handing it in. The students received comments from other students and even faculty at other institutions, which improved their work tremendously. Wiley found that dozens of other people were effectively doing his job for him by providing students with commentary. It multiplied student outcomes without any extra effort on his part. (*http://bit.ly/1MCGrma*)

The University of Maryland Baltimore County found that when they switched chemistry labs from individual students doing experiments and submitting their results, to groups of students posting their findings to a blog and receiving feedback from other students, the average passing rate in class went from 71.2 percent to 85.6 percent, even as the minimum score needed to pass went up. (*https://www.insidehighered.com/news/2009/10/02/chemistry*) Here again students were given the opportunity to identify their errors and correct them before they became a part of the grade.

We can also reduce the fear of public failure. Many faculty in the flipped classroom use class time to pepper students with questions that fish for a specific answer that the instructor has in mind. But this forces the student to guess at what the instructor is thinking, and possibly guess wrong in front of others. Most students decide to leave it to those few who always answer the instructor's questions. Besides, the answer will come out eventually anyway.

When looking for a specific answer, faculty are better off using in-class polling systems to gather responses anonymously. Students are not worried

[handwritten margin note: Everyone gets an "A"]

about guessing wrong, and everyone submits a guess, not just the one student called upon or who raises his or her hand. Having submitted a guess, they can see how others guessed and are interested in discovering whether they got it right. They are now invested in the answer and so are paying better attention to it, and getting it wrong is not a problem.

Consider ways to encourage failure in your online courses.

Reprinted from *Online Classroom*, January 2016.

Continuous Assessments for Better Learning

by John Orlando, Northcentral University

We tend to think of assessments solely as devices for measuring learning. But they also influence how students learn because students will tailor their study strategies to their assessments. This means that you need to think of your assessments as teaching devices themselves.

Naomi Holmes at the University of Northampton tested how assessments influenced learning by comparing learning outcomes and student preferences for a single online assessment at the end of a geography course to short online assessments given weekly during the course. The short assessments were mostly multiple-choice questions, though they sometimes involved short answers. Soon after submitting a weekly quiz, students were also given feedback on whether they had answered questions correctly and why.

One major outcome of the study was that students given weekly tests showed improved grades compared to their single-test peers. The percentage of students achieving the equivalent of a first-class or upper-second-class grade in the module went from 54 percent to 63 percent. As a result, a whopping 82 percent of students preferred the weekly tests, while only 6 percent preferred the term test, with 94 percent of students believing that the weekly quiz format improved their learning.

Students opined about the various ways that the continuous assessments improved their learning. A common view was that the quizzes improved the students' study habits by helping them structure their study. The single assessment at the end of the term allowed students to put off studying to the indefinite future, causing them to lose much of the information that they were given in lectures and readings. Students who were given weekly quizzes were focused on keeping up with material during the course.

Students who took weekly quizzes also showed a marked improvement in their lecture attendance, with the number of students attending all lectures going up from 8 percent to 59 percent. Plus, students taking weekly quizzes were far more likely to review their notes after a lecture. This after-lecture review was critical to learning and something that most students did not consider when the assessment was not looming on the horizon. Some students also said that the quizzes led to spending more time studying overall.

Another finding was that students found the quizzes more stimulating and engaging than the end-of-term assessment. This led them to be more focused during the assessments and to pay more attention to making sure they understood what was taught. It also gave them the feeling of building their knowledge base each week.

Finally, the immediate feedback provided by the weekly assessments allowed students to check their understanding of the material immediately after being introduced to it, which provided them with opportunities to correct any misunderstandings. The feedback also showed them where they were studying incorrectly, allowing them to revise their study habits as they went along. This meant that students could better prepare for the next quiz, which lowered their overall stress when taking the assessments.

It is easy to set up auto-graded quizzes in online courses. While there are many good reasons for including large assessments such as research papers and projects in a course, this study shows that the online instructor can improve learning outcomes by adding short, frequent assessments throughout the course.

Reference

Holmes, Naomi. 2015. Student perceptions of their learning and engagement in response to the use of a continuous e-assessment in an undergraduate module. *Assessment & Evaluation in Higher Education* 40 (1): 1–14.

Reprinted from *Online Classroom*, June 2016.

Reciprocal Feedback in the Online Classroom

by Rob Kelly

Understanding learners' experiences in the online classroom can help you improve your courses for current and future students and help build a strong learning community. Jill Schiefelbein, owner and guru of Impromptu Guru, a company focused on helping individuals and groups improve communication in both face-to-face and online environments, recommends using a reciprocal feedback process to elicit this valuable information from students.

Giving feedback about the learning experience might be new to some students. In order to get students on board with this process, Schiefelbein includes two videos in her courses: one that introduces the instructor and one that explains course expectations. "I make these two separate videos because they are for two very different purposes. I don't want to put them together. I want them to be short and to the point," Schiefelbein says.

These videos are more personal than text announcements and help establish rapport and clearly explain the purpose and benefits of students providing feedback. "Video is a much more personal channel, and people will gravitate to it more than if you [communicate] via email, for example. Once you've established that rapport and that relationship with your students, you can definitely ask for feedback via email because they already feel that they know you," Schiefelbein says.

Follow-through on this feedback is essential. "Actions speak louder than words, and when you say that you're open to a culture of feedback, you need to actually be open to that feedback. You need to be aware that what you're doing may not always be the best way to do things. If you're of the mind-set that what you do is best and nothing is going to change that, then creating a culture of feedback won't be genuine and students will see through that," Schiefelbein says.

Formal feedback

Creating an environment that encourages student feedback is the foundation for actually getting feedback; unless you ask them for specific feedback, it's unlikely that students will be very forthcoming. This is why Schiefelbein asks specific questions when providing feedback to her students.

In each of her courses, Schiefelbein provides quarterly feedback to students, what she refers to as "email check-ins," letting students know where they stand in the course. In these emails, she also asks students the following questions:

- How has your experience been with the organization of the course and the course materials?
- How have you found the discussion questions in helping you understand the course content? Have they been helpful? Why or why not?
- Is there anything else that you'd like to add about your experience in the class? If you're having any difficulties or if you're enjoying a particular part of the course, I'd really love to hear about that.

"I always make sure to ask a yes-or-no question followed by why or why not? It balances quantitative and qualitative feedback. At the very least, students will answer that quantitative question. You'll get some feedback, and the vast majority will also follow up with responses," Schiefelbein says.

Schiefelbein replies to each of these feedback responses from students. In low-enrollment courses, she sends personalized emails. In high-enrollment courses, she uses a form email that says, "Thank you so much for contributing your feedback. This feedback helps me fine-tune this class not only for you but for other students in the future. Thank you for being part of that effort. As always, if you have any questions, please continue to ask."

Informal feedback

Beyond the quarterly check-ins, Schiefelbein recommends checking in less formally at regular intervals, which "lets the students know that I care about them as individuals, not just [as] numbers who are enrolled in the course."

One way she accomplishes this is through engaging with students in "hallway conversations." Each of Schiefelbein's online courses has an area where these informal conversations take place. "It's supposed to mimic what students might talk about in the hallway before class starts or after class ends," she says.

When topics come up in these hallway conversations, Schiefelbein will mention them in a text or voice announcement. "I'll post an announcement that says, 'Check out the hallway conversation area and chime in on the discussion about …' and I'll give the subject line of whatever discussion is relevant. A more organic type of feedback emerges."

In some instances, students will use these hallways conversations to ask one other about assignments or topics that they are struggling with. Schiefelbein responds to these questions and asks other students to share their experiences or offer help. And because of the culture that she fosters in the course, students respond. "Once you foster this community of feedback, you have other students chiming in, feeling a part of this community, feeling this reciprocal relationship with the instructor and with other students in the class and wanting one other to succeed. If you have students in this culture of feedback you've created actively participating, it really works to foster that sense of community, and I've had many students comment that they feel that they had more input, more agency, and more control over their learning. And I think when students feel that they are in control of their learning, they feel that they have more responsibility to do that learning."

Audiovisual feedback

Another way that Schiefelbein elicits student feedback is by inviting them to offer their comments and suggestions via audio and video. (Because of the extra effort involved, she offers students extra credit for doing this.) "It's nice because I get to see them. It establishes a more personal connection with the students. It's surprising to me with some of the better students I've had just how much of a connection I can build via email; however, being able to hear their voices and see their faces just makes the relationship grow even more," she says.

In addition to helping strengthen relationships, the audiovisual format can improve the quality of the feedback. "When a student is putting a video out there that may be viewed by other people, I believe it causes him or her to think more critically about what he or she is saying. And I think that's very beneficial. You can put something on a discussion board in 30 seconds, but if you're going to be on camera, you're going to think more consciously about what you're saying and what you're contributing. It takes some of that anonymity out of the equation. Once you put an image or likeness or voice behind that feedback, it gets a little more real for them, and you have less of an anonymous presence," Schiefelbein says.

Benefits of student feedback

Opening your teaching and course design to student critique can be a daunting prospect, but doing so strengthens the learning community, and students provide information and suggestions that can improve the learning for current and future students. "I was initially scared by what type of feedback would come back to me. I didn't want to open a Pandora's Box when I started this. What I found when I got over that and started asking for feedback was that the comments I received from students, both positive and negative, were communicated respectfully. Students felt agency. They felt more involved in the class," Schiefelbein says.

Student suggestions can also save time. For example, Schiefelbein produced a video to provide students with assignment guidelines. It turned out that students thought that a simple bulleted list would have been more effective, something she might not have become aware of if she had not fostered a culture of reciprocal feedback.

Reprinted from *Online Classroom*, June 2012.

The Benefits of Peer Review

by John Orlando, Northcentral University

Cultivating student creativity is more and more being touted as a fundamental objective of education. We are also hearing more and more about the benefits of peer review activities for student learning. However, some have claimed that peer review of student work dampens creativity (Hurlburt 2008). They argue that student anxiety about how they will appear to others tends to cause them to withdraw into producing less risky work.

Can peer review coexist with creativity? The answer is yes. Liu (2016) and fellow researchers recently found that peer review actually improves student creativity when done correctly. They set up a digital storytelling activity that required one group of students to provide feedback on each other's work and another group to create the stories without receiving feedback from others. The researchers found that the group receiving feedback outperformed the other group on a variety of measures, including overall quality, accuracy, and creativity of their work. Moreover, those who provided feedback also improved their own work.

Another benefit of peer review found in the study was that it helped students better understand their own creativity. Students were asked a series of questions after the activity to measure their creative self-efficacy, essentially their knowledge of their own creativity. Their scores where then compared to the actual creativity demonstrated in their works. The group without peer feedback showed no correlation between the two, while the students in the peer review group showed a match between their self-perception of their creativity and their actual creativity. This coheres with other studies that have found that creative self-efficacy is heavily influenced by social interactions. In other words, we learn about our own creativity from others.

But the most important aspect of the study was that the group pro- *give students*
viding peer feedback was given a rubric to guide their commentary. This, *a rubric to*
it appears, is critical to channeling peer feedback in a positive direction. *guide peer*
Unfortunately, the researchers did not provide more information about *evaluation*
why this is the case, but we might speculate that a rubric helped keep the
feedback on task and helpful to the student. The rubric might prevent the
feedback from drifting into commentary that could be taken poorly by the
student and thus cause him or her to withdraw.

This study suggests that faculty members using peer review can benefit
by providing students with some instruction on how to provide feedback
to their fellow students. Too often I see faculty simply tell students to provide commentary on each other's work, or just give word count parameters,
without any direction on the form of that commentary. It is easy to forget
that students are not used to providing one another with commentary.
Some might even become too timid in fear of hurting another student's
feelings.

One option is to have students apply the same rubric that you use to
evaluate student work. You can make a short screencast of yourself applying
feedback to a sample student work. Draw up the rubric on the screen and
talk through how you interpret each category and also demonstrate how
it is applied to an assignment and what you would say to a student. This
gives the students a sense of direction and confidence to guide their own
feedback.

Students can be given the rubric as a Word document with tables.
Students pick the box in each category that they think applies to other students' work, shades it in, and then provides commentary on what they saw
within the work that led them to the judgement. The intermediary of the
rubric puts needed personal distance between the students, which can remove some of the anxiety suffered by reviewer and receiver alike.

Students can even make screencasts of themselves applying the rubric
using software such as Jing. The student pulls up both the rubric and the
other student's assignment on the screen, talks about which box they put
the work in for each category and why, and goes back into the assignment
to show where they found particular elements that led them to their choices.
The student uploads the result to Jing's free hosting site and sends the other
student the link. This makes the feedback more like a conversation than a
grading activity.

Including a rubric and instructions on how to apply it will ensure that
the peer feedback is used by students to support, rather than judge, one
another. Faculty should explain that good feedback is given with an eye

towards helping the other person see how they can improve their performance. Students should be told to not just find problems but also to suggest solutions, and they will go out of their way to help one another see ways to improve.

References

Hurlburt, S. 2008. Defining tools for a new learning space: Writing and reading class blogs. *MERLOT Journal of Online Learning and Teaching* 4 (2): 182–189.

Liu, C.C., et al. 2016. The impact of peer review on creative self-efficacy and learning performance in web 2.0 learning activities. *Educational Technology & Society 19* (2): 286–297.

Reprinted from *Online Classroom*, July 2016.

Interactive Self-Checks*

by Hannah Digges Elliott, Audrey Anton, and Andrew Swanson, Western Kentucky University

Many online courses still use static content such as readings, PowerPoint presentations, and the like. Students are not "doing" anything other than consuming the information.

We wanted to buck this trend by providing more interactive and engaging content. We did so by creating the Conversations with . . . Aristotle learning module, an interaction that allows students to have a "conversation" with a philosopher and answer a question about it afterward. Students work in an animated environment where they can compare their answers against the philosopher's and express themselves in a fun and interactive way that resembles the video game and role-playing scenarios they so often use recreationally.

When students enter the interaction, Aristotle greets them and asks whether they are familiar with his Nicomachean Ethics. If they indicate that they are, he then asks them to explain his Doctrine of the Mean (feigning to have forgotten it himself, since it's been so long since he wrote it!). The students then type in an essay response explaining the doctrine of the mean. Once this is answered, Aristotle declares that he's found his manuscript! He asks the students to compare their answer to his (the answer is actually Dr. Anton's summary of the topic). Finally, Aristotle asks how similar the two responses were, and makes suggestions of what to review in the event that the responses weren't terribly similar.

Creating the module

We wanted to do a number of things in this module:
- Give students the opportunity to practice answering essay questions.
- Present students with a model of a good essay question.
- Allow students the opportunity to evaluate their answers against the

sample response.
- Take the students outside our learning management system to make the module feel less like a practice test.
- Give students a low-stakes way to be wrong.
- Give students a practice opportunity without creating more grading work for the faculty member.

Before designing the activity, the faculty member first identified areas in her lessons in which students struggled. For example, students in her face-to-face courses have had difficulty grasping aspects of Aristotle's Doctrine of the Mean. Typically, she spent an entire day discussing examples of this principle, with students working in small groups tasked with discerning the appropriate virtue called for, its corresponding vices, and how to determine the "relativity" of the mean to the situation. Indeed, if the concept is usually part of in-class group work, or if the discussion in class is crucial to a student's ability to write an upcoming paper, that might be a good topic to select for an assessment.

Since Dr. Anton's online students were not going to have the luxury of in-class discussion to work through such exercises, we decided to create a formative assessment that gave students the opportunity to answer potential essay exam questions, "get their wrong in," and see what a model answer to the question might look like. These interactions were ungraded, and students had unlimited attempts to practice. What's more, the assessments were designed to be fun. The assessments allowed students to "interact" with philosophers through a simulated conversation, thereby creating the impression that the student is participating in a sort of online game. Basically, students enter the interaction and Aristotle begins speaking to them. As they move through the activity, they respond to his prompts either through written text or button clicking.

We created the interaction by combining Adobe After Effects with Articulate Storyline. After Effects is a program that allows users to create moving animations with audio, and provides the flexibility to create a wide variety of animations. We used it to create features such as a talking philosopher head and an arrow shooting at a tree. Take a look at the After Effects Animation Demonstration (http://bit.ly/1NJvpvK) to see how instructional designer Andrew Swanson created the interactions.

Once we had the animations, we turned to Articulate Storyline to create the interaction. Articulate Storyline is an interactive e-learning content development system. The developer creates slides that utilize interactions and can branch to other slides depending on what the user does. The developer can also create complicated motion paths, embed animation and video, overlay audio, embed quizzes, and do many other things with Articulate Storyline. Plus, it can retain student answers to be used in other slides, and can record information such as attempts in our learning management system (Blackboard).

Combining After Effects and Articulate Storyline allowed us to create an engaging interaction that met all of our learning goals.

Reprinted from *Online Classroom*, April 2016.

Free Clickers for All: Using Google Forms to Survey your Students

by Michael J. LaGier, Grand View University

Like many educators, I am interested in exploring methods that provide real-time, formative assessment in the classroom. Being a teacher of such courses as microbiology, microbial genomics, and immunology, which are dense in jargon and abstract concepts, I need to be able to quickly get a snapshot of how well my students are grasping important ideas or concepts. My students also need this information in order to assess their own learning. To this end, I started exploring the use of personal response systems, or clickers, as a method for rapid classroom assessment. The overall trend of the SoTL data gathered on this topic indicates that clickers can be used for formative assessment, including in my own field of biology. Awesome!

Wait a second. I need to ask my students to spend more of their limited cash on something that resembles technology from ancient times and, unlike many modern electronics, has no other purpose outside class beyond being a paperweight? As someone who had to serve frozen yogurt at the campus dining hall just to scrape together enough money for textbooks and laboratory goggles when I was a student, this struck a negative chord with me.

Okay, I thought, there must be cheaper alternatives. Yes, there are. For example, one might use Poll Everywhere in combination with smartphones as a proxy for clickers. Of course, a downside to Poll Everywhere and its competitors is that the free versions of the software are often stripped-down adaptations of the full, subscription-based accounts. Feeling quite frustrated, I turned to that all-knowing entity of the modern world, Google.

Within Google Drive, I discovered an online survey tool called Google

Forms. With Google Forms I am able to create surveys that my students can answer in real time, for free, using any device that is Wi-Fi compatible and has an Internet browser capable of running Google (smartphones, tablets, and laptops all work). To make a survey within Google Drive, create a new document, and from the subsequent pull-down menu, select "Google Forms" (under "More," the purple icon). Surveys can be anonymous, or you can ask for names to track individual students' progress over time.

The survey questions can be written in a variety of formats, including multiple choice, text, and Likert-type scale. Once the survey is complete, I invite students to participate by providing them a hyperlink via email. I send the hyperlink before each class, encouraging my students to come to class prepared and ready to participate. Alternatively, students can be invited to participate using social media such as Twitter, Google+, or Facebook.

In class, students access the survey via the provided hyperlink, and collective, anonymous, results are shared in real time via the "Summary of responses" choice (use the pull-down menu within the Responses tab of Google Forms). Prior to class, I open the desired Google Forms document (the actual survey) within Google Drive and make sure that the survey is accepting responses (Responses tab). In addition to documenting the collective data from a survey, the software also archives individual responses as an Excel worksheet.

My use of Google Forms as a cheap, easy-to-use, device-friendly alternative to clickers has been yielding some successful results. First, my students look forward to getting the links and love how they can use devices that they already have in order to participate. Preliminary, indirect measures of learning, in the form of post-course student surveys, indicate that the use of Google Forms is helping my students learn better. Finally, I have recently started to use the software not only to ask content and concept-type questions but also to track whether my students' perceptions about important, course-related issues change as the semester progresses. For example, in my microbiology course I use Google Forms surveys to assess whether student attitudes toward the problem of antibiotic resistance change over time.

Reference
Preszler, R. W. et al. 2007. Assessment of the effects of student response systems on student learning and attitudes over a broad range of biology courses. *CBE-Life Sci. Educ.* 6: 29–41.

Reprinted from *Faculty Focus,* January 22, 2016.

Using Verbal Data Analysis and Presentation Software to Construct Group Feedback

by Judy D'Ammasso Tarbox, Southern Connecticut State University

Feedback is one of the most critical components in any classroom. It is especially important in online or distance education and can make the difference between a student feeling positive and student feeling negative about a course. Unfortunately, most of the time "feedback" refers to "what the instructor writes on and about student work product" (Woolsey 2008).

More recent studies have expanded notions of feedback to include "messages without academic content" and "messages with academic content." The former refers to administrative messages that give pertinent information and direction to students—I call them "housekeeping" messages; affective messages that acknowledge student participation and offer support; and public relations types of messages that tell students what might be happening on campus, in a webinar, and so on. The latter are corrective feedback messages on assignments; informative messages that are directed at students' general blog or discussion posts and are aimed personally to each student; and Socratic types of messages that give feedback to individual posts and direct students to think outside of the box, expand further, etc. (Liu 2009).

These are all excellent forms of feedback and do improve student satisfaction with online learning. There is one other type of feedback, however, that has not been mentioned. That is *group* feedback to online asynchronous chat discussion. By using simple methods of verbal data analysis coupled with presentation software, it is possible for instructors to create feedback for asynchronous group discussions that enhance overall learning in the classroom and create a sense of community.

Discussion boards in the form of blogs, journals, and asynchronous chat are part of the de facto standard in learning management software. Asynchronous chat is especially common as a way to create group discussion in an online classroom. Students are expected to post on the discussion board and comment on a certain number of fellow students' posts—I typically use three to five as the number of responses required. What generally happens next is that instructors read all the posts and responses and comment on various posts individually. These feedback interactions are the "informative" or "Socratic" message types discussed above (Liu 2009). I used this method for a while until I found, as I was reading, that there were patterns developing over the course of the discussion—patterns that could improve overall "class discussion" if only each student was reading every post plus responses (not likely). I realized there was a huge untapped potential to expand and improve the efficacy of the discussion. But how to do this efficiently? I decided that since I was dealing with "streams of language" or "verbal data" I would look at methods of capturing and analyzing these phenomena more effectively. So I turned to verbal data analysis techniques used in research. In short, I decided to turn research methods into classroom pedagogy.

Data analysis process

In her book *Analyzing Streams of Language* Cheryl Geisler discusses the importance and prevalence of the "phenomena of language" that are verbal data. She defines them as "data made up of words, often in a continuous stream" and indicates that they include oral interactions in the form of transcribed texts, written interactions in the form of printed texts, and electronic interactions in the form of digital online texts (Geisler 2004). Not wanting to make each weekly discussion a research project, I went through Geisler's methods and adapted them to the format of the classroom. There are five basic steps that I adapted: anchor the work, segment the data, code the data, see data patterns, and present the data.

Step 1: Anchor the work

Geisler's methods start with "finding an anchor point" to ground the research. This is a "foundational work" that would "make a good starting point for an ongoing line of research" and must "be based on an analysis of verbal data...which may be claims about verbal phenomena themselves or claims about other kinds of phenomena, but which can be verified by looking at verbal data" (Geisler 2004).

In the classroom scenario I attach specific materials or tasks to each discussion assignment rather than just having students respond to a question. The anchor point then consists of these artifacts that make up the discussion assignment, along with the students' written discussion posts plus responses.

For example, in a business writing class discussion on "communication strategies" I use two recent articles from business publications. The first discusses overall strategies for employee communication, and the second discusses the importance of written communication in business and professional environments. Both deal with some form of verbal data as the main phenomenon.

In a class on multimedia writing I have the students compare and contrast a specific task that can be done in the digital world as well as the non-digital world. For example, reading print newspapers versus reading their online counterparts. In this case the assignment deals with phenomena that can be verified by looking at verbal data—students creating a written record of their individual experiences and reactions to those experiences. The next step in the classroom paradigm after the students read or work the task is to write a few paragraphs on their readings or experiences. They post their work and respond to classmates. This leads to the second step, segmentation of data.

Step 2: Segment the data

Another of Geisler's main steps is segmentation of the data. She states that "the analysis of verbal data begins when we segment the data into some unit for analysis" (Geisler 2004). This can be a bit complicated in a research paradigm, but in our simple classroom scenario the data is segmented by each student's main post. The responses connected to this become part of that whole segment of data. I read each post and its responses and begin to organize and categorize the data accordingly. Until recently this process was the most low-tech part of the procedure, as I simply jotted down the student's name and noted his or her main "claims" along with important support or repudiation from the responses to that student's posts. I have recently begun copying and pasting the critical text/data points into a separate document, again along with the name and information from responses. As I work through this process I am able to quickly see categories emerging—specific phenomena or experiences that cross segments. This becomes the next step, forming the code.

Step 3: Code the data

After working through all the data segments, the next step is to "code" or "label" the segments "according to the phenomenon" they represent. In the research paradigm this entails development of a comprehensive coding scheme (Geisler 2004). In the classroom scenario I am able to develop categories of data by simply extrapolating the main issue, topic, claim, etc., that each student writes about in his or her post. Specific words or phrases appear across posts and are then used to form groupings of posts and responses that are looking at similar phenomena. For example, in the business environment discussion some students looked specifically at the webcam strategies while others discussed a company meeting complete with a pancake breakfast. These form the categories of "digital strategies," "face-to-face strategies," and so on. This gives an organization and flow of ideas to the discussion as a whole, not just on one specific student or student plus responses. It also leads to the fourth step, seeing patterns in the data.

Step 4: Patterns in the data

This is where the two paradigms, research methods and classroom pedagogy, significantly divide. The research paradigm at this point deals with "distribution schemes" and statistical analysis of the data, "seeing patterns across the various categories in the original analytic design" (Geisler 2004). In the classroom scenario it is possible to recognize patterns by a simple compare and contrast analysis *within* the various groupings and *between* the various groupings created in the coding scheme. How many students were mainly concerned with "digital strategies" as opposed to "nondigital strategies"? Did their responses give any clues as to why they reacted the way they did? Were there any similarities across the groupings? What were these? Was there an overarching pattern that emerged across all or most groupings? If so, how could it be expanded on to explore new dimensions of the discussion assignment?

For example, in the business strategies discussion, many students' responses were concerned with specific tools or artifacts, regardless of whether they were digital or nondigital. This provided a common thread and prompted me, through my feedback presentation, to include information on activity theory and how it fit into the business and professional environment. In the multimedia discussion many students raised issues regarding areas of design and format. This prompted me to include information on visual literacy and usability concepts in the feedback presentation. Once patterns are established, the last stage in the process is to pull together a group feedback presentation that discusses the patterns and creates a sense of community across the segments (students).

Step 5: Present data

The last step in this process is to create a presentation using software that presents the class discussion as a whole while creating a sense of community. I develop the presentation by having an introductory slide that reiterates the assignment. Then I give an overview of the categories that emerged, and I work through each of these. I bring in specific posts, such as "Bill thought the pancake breakfast was interesting but not a sustainable strategy: (cut and paste post from Bill). However, Anne disagreed and said: (insert post from Anne)," and so on.

I weave my way through the categories, creating a narrative and adding additional information, such as information on usability or activity theory, if a common pattern was discovered. This accomplishes three things.

First, it shows students that the instructor is indeed actively involved in their classroom discussions while not directly being inserted into the main feed. Second, it allows the instructor to add to or redirect discussions as warranted. Third, it gives an informative overview of the full discussion so students can see what all their peers are saying and doing even if they have not read every post and response. This creates a sense of community among the class as a whole.

In addition, while I am describing this technique as a valuable tool for the online classroom, I have actually used it in face-to-face classes as well. Again, as previously stated, the asynchronous chat feature is an integral part of learning management software. Therefore, it can also be used as a tool in the face-to-face classroom environment. I use the same assignments for my face-to-face classes and create the same feedback presentations as for my online classes. The difference is that the feedback presentation is shown in class, and is used to prompt a face-to-face discussion. In this situation, students, quite used to "texting" and "posting," are taking the electronic communication and working with it in a face-to-face scenario.

Summary

Feedback in online courses needs to be studied if we are to improve the overall efficacy and satisfaction of classes for students. Various types of feedback—both academic and nonacademic in nature—are being studied and improved. However, these are one-on-one types of feedback between the student and the instructor. One type of feedback, group feedback, appears to be missing from the equation even though group discussion tools are an integral part of learning management systems. Therefore, verbal data analysis techniques provide a method of organizing and analyzing student discussion into a comprehensive form of group feedback. Presentation software provides a platform for the feedback so the entire classroom community can view what their peers are saying while allowing the instructor to expand on concepts that will improve the overall efficacy of the discussion. What is equally nice is that these same techniques can be used in a face-to-face setting, enabling students to go from online text to face-to-face usage of this digital text within the classroom community.

Reprinted from *Online Classroom*, April 2011.

Increase Grading Efficiency with a Comment Archive

by Allen D. Meyer, Liberty University

One of the big challenges of teaching an online course is managing workload while providing the support and feedback that is essential to student success. A good way to become more efficient is to build an archive of grading comments to reduce the time it takes to provide feedback on assignments. By creating an archive, an instructor could insert a comment such as the following with a single keystroke:

> *Keep in mind that APA requires a paragraph to contain at least three sentences.*

With another keystroke, the instructor could add the following:

> *In your application section, you provided some general comments, but make sure to offer specific applications from main points of the article for a specific setting and specific problems. Refer to main concepts from the article, and cite them correctly.*

There are several ways to do this. At Liberty University, one of our residential professors puts his comments on the word processor's clipboard and then inserts them in appropriate places as he is grading papers. Microsoft Word also has a feature called Quick Parts (under the Insert tab) into which you can insert auto text for repeated use. Programs such as APA Grade Assist also provide stock grading comments for numerous writing and APA applications. However, my preferred way of building and inserting archived grading comments is through Word's AutoCorrect option.

You probably already know that Word has numerous auto corrections already programmed. So if you misspell a common word, Word will automatically correct it for you. How, then, would you use that process for building your archive of grading comments?

One of our professors has countless "evaluative" comments to use as he grades a paper, such as this:

The first section provides the foundation of your paper. In the first section, you need to provide a solid overview of the article. The second two sections are reflections on and applications of the article. Without a solid review of the article, the rest of your paper suffers, as was true here.

This same professor also has hundreds of shorter corrections and comments built in using the AutoCorrect feature, such as the following:

Per APA, papers require a general heading, but the introduction section does not have a heading.

The running heading is constructed using the Word header function.

Please review headings, per APA. You also might want to review the levels of headings.

Putting comments into your AutoCorrect file is easy, though building your archive will take some time (which will increasingly pay off in grading efficiency!). Here is one way to build your archive:

1. Highlight the comment you want to archive.
2. Click on File in Word 2010.
3. Click on Options.
4. Choose Proofing.
5. Click on the "AutoCorrect Options" box.

In the Replace box, type a short abbreviation of the grading comment, which can be a short word description—anything that will identify the comment for you. Some professors keep a categorized list of their shortcuts, organized by topic (writing, content, APA, etc.), but as you use the comments repeatedly, you will remember the common shortcuts.

No matter how you do it, building an archive of grading comments is essential to increasing your grading efficiency without sacrificing grading quality and without sacrificing grading that is individualized to the student.

Reprinted from *Online Classroom,* July 2012.

CHAPTER 4

•

Communication Strategies for the Online Classroom

Which Assessment Strategies Do Students Prefer?

by John Orlando, Northcentral University

While most faculty stick with the tried-and-true quiz and paper assessment strategies for their online courses, the wide range of technologies available today offers a variety of assessment options beyond the traditional forms. But what do students think of these different forms?

Scott Bailey, Stacy Hendricks, and Stephanie Applewhite of Stephen F. Austin State University experimented with different assessment strategies in two online courses in educational leadership, and surveyed students afterward on their impressions of each one. The students were asked to score the strategies using three criteria: enjoyment, engagement with the material, and transferability of knowledge gained to practice. The resulting votes allowed investigators to rank the various strategies from least to most preferred by students.

Interestingly, scores for the three criteria were remarkably consistent within each strategy. Students who found an activity highly enjoyable normally found it engaging and with a high degree of transferability of knowledge and vice versa. Moreover, traditional forms of assessment tended to score near the bottom.

The rankings provide a guide for any faculty member looking to develop engaging online content. Below are the different strategies grouped from lowest to highest in preference.

Lowest

1. Quizzes were by far the lowest-ranked assessments on the list.

Very few students found the information transferable to other environments.

2. Traditional papers between two and eight pages long scored higher than quizzes, but were still near the bottom of the list.

3. Group projects were also ranked low on the list. Students were asked to collaborate on a series of tasks and submit a written paper on the outcome of their efforts. While faculty assign these to teach collaboration skills, students often see them as creating additional coordination work and the free rider problem.

Middle

1. Audio recordings fell into a middle category. Students created recordings of themselves explaining course concepts as they would to parents, faculty, or other groups. While some students were initially hesitant about the technology, they quickly picked up the systems and generally enjoyed the activity.

2. Open discussion involved students posting to the traditional course discussion forum on their LMS. Students generally valued open discussion, but it is important to structure it in a way that provides interesting and thought-provoking questions.

3. Paired discussion was a variation on the traditional discussion in which students posted messages on course room boards in groups of two to five. The ratings for these group discussions were similar to those for course wide discussions.

Highest

1. Response to video was at the top of the list. Here students watched a video documentary and responded with a written analysis. Students found the video documentary inspiring and moving. They connected with it on a more emotional level than they would a reading, as it provided a real-world connection to the material. An instructor can find a wide range of excellent documentaries to include in courses from sites such as Free Documentaries TV.

2. Twitter summaries came in as the second most preferred form of assessment. Students were required to summarize in a tweet each of the chapters that they read. By being limited to 140 characters or fewer, the exercise helped students distill main points down to central themes, which is important for synthesizing points in the material.

3. Screencasts were the next most highly ranked types of assessments.

The students created mock presentations that they would give as new administrators to the faculty of a school. The screencasts included both the presentation material and a corner webcam video of the students themselves delivering the narration. Free systems such as Screencast-o-matic are ideal for creating screencasts that combine computer display with webcam videos. The basic format can be applied to a variety of subjects and assignments, such as students in a history course doing a mock presentation to a local historical society on a famous event.

4. Field experiences involved students taking part in an experience related to the course content. This serves as a reminder that even online students can be given assignments that require some sort of fieldwork. It might be to catalog fauna in a local park for a biology class, or to report on local bridge structures for a civil engineering course.

5. Interviews of local school administrators were also popular. Students interviewed two administrators and created a reflection on what they learned about the positions. Once again, these interviews connected the course material with practice.

6. Work samples provided students with an opportunity to take a given data set or scenario and produce a document similar to one they would create as practitioners in their field. These could be professional development plans for their faculty, campus needs assessments, etc. These provided an opportunity for students to apply what they learn to a professional situation.

Themes

The student preferences suggest a few principles that can guide an instructor in choosing assessments for an online course. For one, the mere fact that students were given something beyond the same old papers and quizzes created engagement. Novelty itself can be a reason for choosing an assessment activity. Two, assignments that allow students to apply their knowledge to real or hypothetical scenarios are preferred over academic exercises that just ask students to repeat what they know. These application activities are often called "authentic" assessments, as they mimic how the student will be using their knowledge in the future. Three, an engaging assessment is often a result of engaging content. Even good old-fashioned written assignments were viewed favorably when they were based on an engaging video.

Use these results to choose engaging assessments for your online courses.

Reference

Bailey, S., S. Hendricks, and S. Applewhite. 2015. Student perspectives of assessment strategies in online courses. *Journal of Interactive Online Learning* 13 (3): 112–25.

Reprinted from *Online Classroom*, January 2016.

Selecting the Appropriate Communication Tools

by Rob Kelly

When designing an online course, it's important to carefully consider which tools align with the course's learning objectives and the types of communication that will occur.

There are three types of communication that can occur in an online course—one to one, one to many, and many to many. In an interview with *Online Classroom*, Sara Ombres, faculty development instructor, and Anna Reese, production coordinator/instructional designer, both at Embry-Riddle Aeronautical University's Worldwide Campus, talked about how they help instructors select communication tools to suit the situation.

One to one: journals

A key strength of online learning is the ability to create learning communities, facilitate collaboration, and foster peer review. However, there are instances where one-to-one communication is appropriate. For example, a journal that only the individual student and instructor can access can be used as a way for students to reflect on sensitive topics in a less public way than using other tools might offer. Or in a writing course, perhaps students would prefer not to share their work with the entire class until they've made revisions.

In addition to being useful to the students, one-to-one communication can provide valuable information to the instructor.

"We have students journal about what they're struggling with—things they may not feel comfortable sharing with the group. It's really good feedback for us as faculty developers and instructors to modify and improve [our instruction] to better meet their needs," Ombres says.

One to many: blogs

Consider using blogs as a way to provide students with a means to communicate to the entire class. Although blogs can be set up to enable comments from other students, they're not the best tool for interactive discussion. Rather, they are an excellent way for individual students to share their personal experiences, reflect, and apply what they've learned, Reese says.

Blogs provide a sense of ownership. "Students can comment on other students' blogs, but they cannot add posts to other students' blogs. The blog is the individual student's to do what he or she wants to do. And there has been a lot of research about how when students have that feeling of ownership it really does improve their writing and their level of commitment," Ombres says.

Blogs also enable the instructor to clearly see the contributions and are good for tracking students' learning throughout a course or even a program.

"If you're asking the same questions every week, you may find that a blog is more conducive to success than a discussion board because then you're really able to see the individual student's work. You see all their reflections through the whole course. You have all of that one student's posts on one page, and it really allows the students to see their own growth and progression. … It's one to many. Anybody can see it, but it's organized by student rather than by topic," Ombres says.

Each student enrolled in Embry-Riddle's master's-level leadership program keeps a blog throughout the program. "They're supposed to try to correlate what they just learned in that module with something that's going on in their professional careers or something they experienced in the past. Students are encouraged to provide their opinions and thoughts that go along with it. By the time they get through this leadership program, they're going to be able to go through this blog and see how their views changed during the program," Reese says.

Many to many: discussion boards, wikis

The discussion board often is the default communication tool. There are good reasons for this. Discussion boards are easy to use and give everybody the opportunity to contribute. The key to using discussion boards effectively is asking the right type of questions. "I always recommend that if you can, have students relate [the question] to their personal experiences. Having them bring in their own experiences is a very quick and easy way to elevate the discussion board, and that's what really gets the students engaged in participating in the forum," Ombres says.

The discussion board is best suited for many-to-many communication where there is not a single answer to a question or problem. Prompts are typically in the form of open-ended questions, but they don't need to be. Students can respond to any content—a picture, an audio file, a video, etc.

"Some [prompts] lead to really good discussions, and there are some that are just more reflective questions that students think about on their own rather than sharing their opinions and counteracting others' posts. I think [discussion boards] are most appropriate when you want students to learn from each other," Ombres says.

Discussion boards are often informal, but you also can make them more formal in order to suit the goals of the course. For example, you can require students to include three resources in their posts, taking advantage of the asynchronous format by encouraging students to formulate well-informed posts, Ombres says.

Discussion boards can be used for debates and simulations. For example, an aviation law course uses the discussion board for simulating court cases, in which students take turns playing the role of plaintiff, defendant, and judge. The plaintiff and defendant each have a week to come up with a case brief and present it to the judge, who posts it on the discussion board for the entire class to debate for a week. The parties then have an opportunity to defend their cases, and after a week the judge makes a ruling.

Wikis also can be used for many-to-many communication, typically for collaborative projects.

"If you're asking a group of students to share their experiences related to topic X, that would be more appropriate for a discussion board. But if you're telling a group of students to create a paper that explains a theory that was discussed in class, then I would use a wiki," Ombres says.

Many online courses at Embry-Riddle feature group projects in which students work together in groups of three or four to create some kind of deliverable—a presentation or paper that they create as a group. Ombres says that wikis have been the best way for students to work on these projects because wikis enable students to work on a single file without having to worry about whether it's the current version. A major difference between a wiki and a discussion board is that a wiki does not really differentiate between individual students' contributions the way discussion boards do. However, wikis do enable the instructor to view individuals' contributions, which helps when assigning grades.

An important consideration

Learning outcomes should be the overriding consideration when selecting and using communication tools, Reese says. "It doesn't matter how flashy the tool is or how excited you are to use it if it's not the right tool for the job. It's important to design with your learning outcomes in mind, figure out what you want your end result to be, and then choose the tool that will help you get there versus picking the tool that you really want to use and then trying to model your course or learning outcomes around that."

Reprinted from *Online Classroom*, November 2012.

Rubric Options for an Online Class

by John Orlando, Northcentral University

Athletes are often "graded out" by their coaches after a game, and they always know ahead of time the exact criteria that will be used to grade them. An offensive lineman knows that he will be graded on the number of sacks allowed, missed blocks, etc. The clear performance criteria allow athletes to focus on meeting them.

Unfortunately, the same is not always true of higher education. As a graduate student, I was taught how to grade students down on essay assignments for various errors. But I was not taught to explain my grading methodology to students ahead of time, so many students' errors were a result of not knowing what I wanted.

Rubrics are an ideal way to clarify expectations for students. The assessment categories are clearly laid out and the different performance levels within each category demonstrate what constitutes good or bad performance. Rubrics provide students with models of what to do and what to avoid. This helps guide them in developing their work.

Rubrics also make the grading process easier by breaking it down into discrete items. The teacher has a clearer picture of what to look for. Plus, the rubric helps keep the instructor on track after doing a number of assignments. We all wonder about the "grading drift" that causes us to grade harder or easier as we get farther into a pile of assignments. Some instructors will even regrade an earlier assignment at the end to see whether they have drifted. Rubrics limit drift by tethering us to a standard.

But rubrics are also helpful in developing the assessment itself. Faculty normally consider assessments after determining their course content. But many educational theorists want faculty to reverse this process by first determining how students will be assessed, and then developing content that teaches to those assessments. While the term "teaching to the test" is often used pejoratively, it actually makes perfect sense. If the player will be assessed on how many sacks he gives up, then his training should focus on how not to give up sacks.

Starting with an assessment rubric also helps clarify in the instructor's mind what he or she wants students to learn, and thus what should be taught. If critical thinking is an important part of the rubric, then the instructor needs to make sure that it is covered in the class. Too often students are graded on general skills like critical thinking without any explicate or related teaching, as if they were to acquire them by osmosis. It is a good exercise to sketch out in a rubric exactly what criteria will be used to grade students, and then compare it to your course content to see whether you cover all of those skills.

Rubric Software

While many faculty build their rubrics in an Excel or Word document, there are a number of free online systems that make the process much easier. These all function in similar ways. Each provides a template in which you define the performance categories as rows and levels of performance within each category as columns, and then fill in the boxes at each intersection of the two.

iRubric (*www.rcampus.com/indexrubric.cfm*) is a simple and powerful tool from RCampus. One nice feature of the site is that there is a gallery of over 485,000 rubrics made by other teachers that you can use or modify for your own purposes. I did a search on "digital storytelling" and came up with over 3,000 rubrics, and so there should be something for nearly any purpose. After creating your rubric, you can copy and paste it into a Word document as a table that you then copy onto a student's work. I like to highlight the boxes that correspond to the student's performance with a background color after copying the rubric into the assignment to make it clear what determined the student's grade. If you wish to pay for the premium version, you can enter students into the system and have your choices automatically calculated and graded. For tutorial see (*https://youtu.be/JmNhEelN4o0*).

OrangeSlice (*http://bit.ly/1KUAiXt*) is a free Google Docs add-on that you can incorporate into your Chrome browser. You open a student's work in Docs, open the rubric, and highlight boxes. OrangeSlice will calculate the scores and provide the student with a grade. This is ideal for faculty having students submit their work in Google Drive.

QuickRubric (*www.quickrubric.com*) is another simple yet powerful rubric-making tool. It works similarly to iRubric in that it provides a template with columns and rows to fill in. Unlike iRubric, it does not have a gallery of rubrics, but it does have a Tips to Writing a Strong Rubric page that can provide a good guide to getting started with rubrics. Plus, as a stand-alone system without a suite of non-rubric features, it presents a less cluttered page to work on if you are just interested in creating a rubric from scratch.

Try any of these rubric options to improve your grading and students' performance.

Reprinted from *Online Classroom*, February 2016.

Reduce Online Course Anxiety with a Check-in Quiz

by Maryellen Weimer, Penn State Berks

"Online classes are often intimidating for first-time students," writes David St Clair. "They wrestle with the gnawing fear that their class has no anchor in the physical world and that there will be no one there to address their fears and concerns" (St Clair 2015, 129). His solution? A simple, online check-in quiz.

Here's how the activity unfolds. The first assignment in the online course, to be completed on the first day, is this required check-in quiz. In St Clair's case, it meets the university's first-day attendance requirement. Students can be dropped from the course if they don't meet that university requirement. They read the syllabus and take the quiz, which comes to them as an attachment in the course welcome email. The quiz is also posted on the course Blackboard site. Beyond fulfilling the check-in requirement, this quiz is actually a tour of course features. "To find the quiz, learn about the quiz, take the quiz, and to receive their grade on the quiz, students need to navigate through virtually every part of the online class site" (St Clair 2015, 130). As St Clair points out, you could "tell" students how to navigate the features of the online course, but the more powerful way is having them discover those features for themselves.

Based on his experience, here's an abbreviated set of features St Clair has found contribute to the success of this activity.

Require the quiz

It's a graded assignment, not something students do for extra credit. At the very beginning of a course, most students don't think they need extra credit. However, this should be a low-stakes assignment, worth a nominal number of points, but with the risk of a serious penalty if left incomplete.

It's a first assignment

"Online classes must engage students quickly and get them into a class rhythm." (St Clair 2015, 131) This early engagement is even more critical for students new to online learning.

Announce it in the announcements

The quiz should be announced prominently so that it can't be missed. That also starts to establish course routines: announcements like this one precede every exam and assignment in the course.

Make it short and simple

The goal is to take students to all the critical places in the course, not to answer every question they might have about the course. A short quiz more effectively focuses students on the process, not the content, and short quizzes are less intimidating.

It's not a course content quiz

This quiz does not assess background knowledge—that increases anxiety. Rather, it prepares students for learning in the online environment generally and in this course specifically.

Syllabus items make good content for a check-in quiz

What's the grading policy in this course? Where do you find your course grades? Do you submit drafts of your papers? What's the procedure for doing so? Where are the course readings located?

The quiz should be lighthearted or humorous

If the objective is reducing anxiety, a lighthearted approach accomplishes that goal more effectively. Besides helping students relax, humor conveys important messages about the instructor. He or she comes across as an approachable human being.

The quiz should showcase normal course patterns and procedures

In a low-pressure way, the quiz shows students how assessment activities occur in the course. "There's no advantage to introducing students to features that are not part of the course navigation protocol." (St Clair 2015, 132) The same holds true for grading the quiz. The grading processes, including submitting the quiz and finding out the results, should mirror the processes that will be used throughout the course.

The check-in quiz doesn't eliminate all the anxiety new (and not-so-new) students experience—it's not magic, according to St Clair. However, he estimates it reduces the number of anxious emails received from students early in the course by about 80 percent. It's a strategy that sets up students to effectively manage the features of online learning.

Reference

St Clair, D. 2015. A simple suggestion for reducing first-time online student anxiety. *MERLOT Journal of Online Learning and Teaching 11* (1): 129–135.

Reprinted from *The Teaching Professor*, August/September 2015.

Communicating with Students Online: Ideas for Active Learning

by Rob Kelly

Heidi Beezley, instructional technologist at Georgia Perimeter College, strives to instill online courses with active learning, "providing opportunities for students to meaningfully talk and listen, write, read, and reflect on the content, ideas, issues, and concerns of an academic subject" (as defined by Meyers and Jones). To this she adds: "interact[ing] with realia, manipulatives, simulations, etc."

Educators need to take into account the characteristics of the online classroom when trying to incorporate active learning into online courses, Beezley says. For example, the nonlinear nature of the online classroom and the lack of face-to-face interaction with its visual cues make it difficult to ensure that all learners are experiencing the course in the same manner.

"Face-to-face discussions are linear. Everyone has a shared experience. The conversation slowly builds, and hopefully by the end you've moved everyone from one level of understanding to a new level of understanding. In an online environment when you have students participate in a discussion through a discussion board, it's not linear at all. There's not necessarily a shared experience. Everybody reads posts in a different order, or they may not read all of them. There may be no clear building of the conversation, because it's not linear, so it could go in lots of different directions," Beezley says.

Threaded discussion summaries

To help create shared learning experiences, Beezley has students take turns summarizing the threaded discussions. This helps create a common understanding, serves as a means of assessing students' understanding of the content, and gives the chance to actively engage with the course content.

Rather than posting these summaries to the discussion board, Beezley has students post them to a course wiki or to Google Docs. This increases the accessibility of the summaries, which can be important for future reference and to enable all the students to edit them in case the student who did the original summary overlooked or misinterpreted key concepts.

Beezley recommends discussing the summary (synchronously or asynchronously) with the students to assess its accuracy and prevent incorrect information from becoming ingrained in students' minds. "Whenever possible, have students interact with the summary so that they are looking at it critically," Beezley says.

Synchronous collaboration

Beezley is an advocate of synchronous sessions as a way to create active learning opportunities. She uses Wimba, a live classroom program, to facilitate synchronous collaboration, including discussions (chat and/or voice), polling, and breakout rooms in which students can work on shared documents and report back to the entire class.

Beezley prefers to have students actually talk to each other as they collaborate in the breakout rooms. As in a face-to-face classroom, the instructor can visit with each group to ensure that they are going in the right direction.

"If things are going well, I usually leave them to do what they're doing and know that they're going to be reporting back when we meet in the main room. I find that I can usually just be the observer because the conversations are going well. I think the trick is to try to pull them back to the main room before they get to the point where the discussion has died down. Sometimes groups may not be done discussing before you pull them all back and ask them to report on whatever they did. [You need to] establish a culture of accountability, making sure that they need to use the time wisely, or they will run out of time and won't be able to complete the task," Beezley says.

As in the face-to-face classroom, spontaneous off-topic conversations are likely to occur in the synchronous online environment. While too much of this can detract from the learning experience, a certain amount of it is productive. "Some of my best learning in college occurred while walking out of a classroom when the class was over and asking, 'Did you understand this part of the lecture? It was confusing to me.' Conversations like that are hard to have in the online environment. When you put people together in small groups, sometimes they have those kinds of conversations. I think those conversations are a good thing."

To help facilitate these collaborations, Beezley assigns each student to a base group of students who work together throughout the course. "Instead of having one large group, I like the idea of everyone taking part in the same discussion in small groups of five students who are always working together and talking things through and reporting back to the class."

Ready, set, go

As a graduate student, Beezley participated in synchronous sessions facilitated by her instructor Peyri Herrera, who used a technique Beezley calls "Ready, set, go" to actively engage students.

It's a simple understanding check in which the instructor asks students to answer a question in chat and to submit their answers simultaneously on cue. The questions can be simple or complex. They can test recall or higher-order thinking. The key is to have students hit submit simultaneously so everyone's answer is revealed at the same time.

"As a student I really feared that I would be wrong, because when it's live there isn't as much time to think about a response as there would be asynchronously. I think that fear is a healthy thing for students to feel. It raises your level of engagement. It makes you pay attention. It really helped me learn because whenever I was right I felt validated. But when I was wrong, I would pay attention even more.

"When you have that opportunity for the synchronous exchange of ideas, I think the stakes are higher than when it is asynchronous. When it is asynchronous, you have time to think through your responses, and I think that's a good thing to have those times as well, but I think in that asynchronous event you have to think on your feet and apply what you know quickly. As an instructor it's a great opportunity to really see where your students are and understand how much they've learned," Beezley says.

Reprinted from *Online Classroom,* December 2011.

Online Teaching 2.0: Easy Podcasting for the Classroom

by John Orlando, Northcentral University

Podcasts are an easy way to liven up an online course. Podcasts are nothing more than audio files, and have been found to enhance student learning, satisfaction, and feelings of connectedness in online courses.

One use of podcasts is to deliver course content. Instead of writing out a "lecture," an instructor can record it for the students to download and listen to through their cell phones and earbuds while walking to class, riding a bus or bike, driving, etc. Beyond portability, podcasts have been shown to improve the ability to convey nuance in the message, as much of our communication comes through the tone and other inflections in our voice. This is also particularly beneficial for instructors using podcasts to provide feedback on student work, and accounts for much of the universal praise that those podcasts receive from students.

Instructors can also have students make podcasts. Marjorie Chan (2014) had her students record interviews with business leaders for a management class. The interviews were in a live radio format, with the host interviewing a guest, and students calling in with questions. This added an exciting, interactive element to the course. The recordings were then put together into a series that could be added to the course content for the benefit of future students. A department can also create a podcasting series on monthly topics, with interviews of students, faculty, or outside experts.

Another use for podcasts is as a form of assessment. Students can be assigned to make podcasts in an NPR-segment format to explain a topic. The benefit of the radio documentary format over a traditional academic paper is that students are forced to ask what makes the topic interesting, and how to present it in a way that will be understandable to a lay audience, rather than just their instructor. The experience helps them develop communication skills that are relevant in today's digital world.

Recording a podcast

A good entry into podcasting is to simply record your voice for course content, tutorials on course processes, or feedback to a student. One option is to record with the free, open source Audacity program, which is available for download at *Sourceforge*. You can both record and edit your recording directly on *Audacity*, and then export it to be hosted elsewhere.

Recording interviews for a radio show format is not much harder. BlogTalkRadio is a paid service that is designed to create live radio shows. It hosts a live show with multiple callers, and saves a recording to its Web site. The site provides all of the search, cataloging, and publicity functions that you need to run a radio series.

A free alternative to *BlogTalkRadio* is Google's *Hangouts on Air*, a feature of Google+. Hangouts on Air will broadcast live video of up to 10 people at once to YouTube, and automatically create a recording of the outcome as well.

If you only want to record interviews that are not broadcast live, you can use *Skype*. Skype allows free group calls for a small number of users at once. However, it does not come with recording capacity, so you will need to download and run a free Skype recording app such as *MP3 Skype Recorder* or *Pamela Skype Recorder* to record the outcome.

Hosting a podcast

Your Learning Management System might come with podcast hosting capability built in, and if you use BlogTalkRadio, or the video version of the Hangouts on Air broadcast, the website itself will host both the live event and the recording. But if your LMS does not have this capability, or you want to make a podcast available to others outside of the course room—such as for a departmental series—then you will need a way to host it. Luckily, there are a number of free and easy options.

A simple hosting method is to load the podcasts to either a Google Drive or Dropbox account, and provide students with the link. Another possibility is to load them to iTunesU, which is designed for higher education. Your students are likely already familiar with it.

Best practices for making podcasts

Remember that the goal of a podcast is to sound natural, as if you are sitting next to the listener. The problem is that most people tense up in front of a microphone, producing monotone recordings that lull the listener to sleep. You can avoid this result by following a few simple rules.

First, don't slow down. We tend to slow our cadence in front of a microphone because we are unsure of ourselves. But keep in mind that the person listening is not hard of hearing, and so you should speak with the cadence you would use with someone sitting next to you.

Also remember to add the voice inflections that produce emphasis. If you are asking a question, do so in a tone that sounds like you are asking a question. In fact, you should probably overdo the expressiveness, as the listener does not get the facial cues that add emphasis to our speech. Feel free to add the conversational elements that create interest for the listener. Say "wow" or "that's crazy" when appropriate.

As for the recording processes, there is a reason why NPR segments do not last longer than about 15 minutes. Fifteen minutes is the limit of our attention span, and so if your topic is longer than 15 minutes, break it into a sequence of shorter podcasts.

Most important, nothing will drive your listeners away faster than having a hard time hearing the message. Most sound quality problems are the result of a poor microphone. Avoid using the pinhole microphone built into your laptop, which gives a distant tone, usually with static. Instead use a headset microphone. Webcam microphones also generally produce decent sound quality.

If you are not recording a live show, but rather course content, you will want to eliminate errors to make a "clean" recording. Restarting from the beginning every time you make an error will cause your production time to explode. A good trick is to record with an editor such as Audacity, and when you make an error, just pause and start again from the last natural break. Then delete the mistakes using the editor at the end, which will leave the clean runs. The pause creates a flat line on your recording timeline to insert your curser to make the cut.

Consider how podcasted interviews, radio shows, or course content can liven up your online course.

Reference
Chan, M. 2014. The use of BlogTalkRadio in online management classes. *MERLOT Journal of Online Learning and Teaching 10 (3):* 504–23.

Reprinted from *Online Classroom*, August 2015.

A Rising Tide Lifts All Boats: Raising, Communicating, and Enforcing Expectations in Online Courses

by Marie A. Revak, Jones University

As an instructor new to the online environment, I carefully reviewed the syllabus and the requirements for the course discussions and assignments and incorporated the following ideas from Myers-Wylie, Mangieri, and Hardy: a "what you need to know" document that includes policies about late work, formatting, source citations, grading and feedback, and the dangers of plagiarism; a separate "assignments at a glance" calendar that details due dates and submission instructions; a "frequently asked questions" thread in the discussion forum; detailed scoring rubrics for each assignment, and example assignments. As is typical in the online environment, my course was equipped with areas for announcements and discussions and a grade book with a place to post comments for individual students. I used all these formats to communicate with students about course requirements and provide detailed feedback.

From the beginning, some students submitted their assignments without reading any of my sage advice. About a third missed the deadline for the first assignment. Several assignments were missing key components, and some exhibited major formatting flaws. There was a flurry of questions in the discussion forum about the due date and format—answers to which could be found in the numerous documents I had posted. Student frustration mounted when I referred them to existing documents. Indeed, the instant gratification associated with the Internet has "trained students to expect help when they require it—on their schedule" (Creasman 2012).

I provided feedback by electronically editing each assignment and returning the marked-up documents. I was discouraged when I noticed that students continued to make the same errors on subsequent assignments—proof that they had not incorporated my previous feedback. Had they even seen it? It occurred to me that I would need to find more innovative ways to communicate my expectations.

I have been able to raise expectations and improve the quality of work in my course by implementing the following practices.

Set a tone of "no excuses"

According to McKeachie (1994), when students know what to expect, they can be more productive. In addition to introducing themselves at the start of the course, I ask students to answer the following questions: How will you make time for this course? and What is your "plan b" for computer and/or Internet issues? When students answer these questions they are forced to think about potential issues and solutions before the class begins. Reading about how other students tackle these problems is also helpful.

Introduce another voice

Students listen to other students. During the first week of class, I post an announcement that summarizes advice collected from previous students from the preceding class. As a rule, this advice encourages students to keep up with the readings, follow instructions, work hard, and meet deadlines. Seasoned students will also advise new students to pay attention to the examples and rubrics. This advice is especially helpful to students who are fearful or easily discouraged (McKeachie 1994). Students will have the opportunity to provide their own advice at the end of the course.

Force engagement with the information

Online students are pragmatic. They need a reason to seek information, especially information that might not directly relate to an assignment that carries a grade. I created an online scavenger hunt quiz based on the course logistics information and awarded extra credit points based on the quiz score. The quiz consists of 12 multiple-choice questions covering the topics of late work, due dates, grading, feedback, plagiarism, formatting, and the course textbook. Students are permitted to take the quiz as many times as they wish during the first week of class. Because my course is asynchronous, most students take advantage of the extra-credit opportunity and therefore become engaged and familiar with the information within the first week when it is convenient for them. Although the extra-credit points are minimal (six points out of 1,000 course points), most students like starting the course with a few extra points in the grade book.

Force engagement with feedback

Research supports corrective feedback as one of the most powerful ways of enhancing student achievement (Angelo and Cross 1993; Marzano, Pickering, and Pollock 2001; McKeachie 1994). But it is not the giving of feedback that helps students learn, but the acting on feedback (Chappuis 2012). I provide feedback to students by electronically editing their individual documents and placing them in a special feedback thread in the discussion forum. One of my biggest disappointments was providing detailed feedback to students and having them make the same mistakes on subsequent assignments. I was spending hours providing feedback, but many students were not learning from my feedback. In fact, I was not even sure that they had found my feedback. To ensure that students find and open their marked-up assignments, I now include a feedback code on the second major assignment. The code consists of the student's initials and a few numbers (for example, MR456). Students reply to me with their feedback code for a few extra credit points on their next assignment. Most students take advantage of this extra credit opportunity, therefore assuring me that they know where to find their marked-up papers.

Force engagement with peers

Most online courses require weekly discussion postings with responses to classmates. Indeed, "the best online instruction allows for students' learning to be forged more through interaction with each other and less through instructor lecture" (Creasman 2012). To encourage participation and ensure that students don't tune out after they have submitted their minimum number of required postings, I require students to review their classmates' comments and submit a revised, polished version of their original post. The revised version is posted at the end of the week and is the version that is graded. In addition to commenting on content, I ask peers to provide advice on spelling, grammar, and conventions. I also comment on student forum postings throughout the week. According to Bullen (1998), instructors need to allow adequate time for follow-up discussion and comments. McKeachie (1994) agrees; more comments and more specific comments lead to greater learning. Because the feedback for the discussion forum refers to the draft post, it occurs during and not after the learning, and therefore often improves the quality of assignments that are submitted at the end of the week (Chappuis 2012).

Provide student exemplars

My course is project-based, and although the course syllabus describes the expectations and provides criteria for the projects, seeing an example of a well-done project will help, direct, and inspire students in their own projects. Kerr (2009) agrees and feels that exemplars support student success and contribute to the development of the learning community. The first time I taught the course, I created my own exemplars. Now that I have taught the course several times, I share actual student examples (with names removed) as exemplar projects.

Provide opportunities for student-to-teacher feedback

Halfway through the course, I ask students to provide me with feedback about how I might improve the course. I ask three questions: What should I start doing? What should I stop doing? What should I continue doing? (Angelo and Cross 1993). I allow about a week for students to respond, then summarize the results and share with students via the discussion forum. At the end of the course, I ask students the same three questions and one additional question: What advice do you have for future students in this course? The mid-course and end-of-course feedback has helped me shape the course and make subtle changes. As the result of student feedback, I have simplified my late work policy and created an area in the discussion forum for students to share project ideas. I share students' advice for future students and believe it is one of the first steps in setting high expectations for the incoming class.

Taken together, implementing the practices described above has helped to improve the quality of the work submitted by students in my classes by setting high expectations from the first day of class and maintaining high expectations throughout the course. By raising the tide, I have lifted all boats!

References

Angelo, T.A. and K. P. Cross. 1993. *Classroom assessment techniques: A handbook for college teachers.* San Francisco: Jossey-Bass.

Chappuis, J. 2012. How am I doing? *Educational Leadership 70 (1):* 36–41.

Creasman, P. 2012. *Considerations in online course design. IDEA paper no. 52,* Kansas State University Center for Faculty Evaluation and Development.

Duncan, H. 2005. On-line education for practicing professionals: A case study. *Canadian Journal of Education 28* (4): 874–896.

Kerr, C. 2009. Asynchronous online learning communities. *Ontario Action Researcher 10 (2):* 1–20.

Marzano, R.J., D. J. Pickering, and J. E. Pollock. 2001. *Classroom instruction that works: Research-based strategies for increasing student achievement.* Alexandria, VA: Association for Supervision and Curriculum Development.

McKeachie, W.J. 1994. *Teaching tips: Strategies, research, and theory for college and university teachers.* Lexington, MA: D.C. Heath and Company.

Myers-Wylie, D., J. Mangieri, and D. Hardy. 2009. *The in's and out's of online instruction: Transitioning from brick and mortar to online teaching.* Parker, CO: Outskirts Press, Inc.

Reprinted from *Online Classroom*, May 2013.

About the Contributors

Audrey Anton is an assistant professor in philosophy at Western Kentucky University.

Tim J. Bristol is a nurse educator, consultant, and technology specialist. He develops new programming and focuses on instructional design for e-learning. He has authored numerous print and electronic resources.

Gloria P. Craig is a professor in the College of Nursing at South Dakota State University.

Ted Cross is the deputy chief of staff at EdPlus at ASU. Ted earned his BA in English from Brigham Young University and later his MA in English from ASU. He also completed an MSed in Education at the University of Pennsylvania.

Judy D'Ammasso Tarbox is an assistant professor of English at Southern Connecticut State University.

Cindy Decker Raynak is a senior instructional designer at the Schreyer Institute for Teaching Excellence at Penn State University.

Hannah Digges Elliott is an instructional designer in distance learning at Western Kentucky University.

Robert (Rob) Kelly is former editor of the *Academic Leader* and *Online Classroom* newsletters and assisted with *The Teaching Professor* newsletter for Magna Publications.

Michael J. LaGier is an assistant professor of biology at Grand View University.

Jean Mandernach's research focuses on enhancing student learning through innovative online instructional strategies. Jean received her BS in comprehensive psychology from the University of Nebraska at Kearney, an MS in experimental psychology from Western Illinois University, and a PhD in social psychology from the University of Nebraska at Lincoln.

Emily Moore is an instructional design consultant at Boise State University, eCampus Center–Extended Studies.

Jennifer Patterson Lorenzetti is editor of *Academic Leader: The Newsletter for Academic Deans and Department Chairs.* She has worked in and written about higher education for more than 20 years, and is the author of *Lecture Is Not Dead: Ten Tips for Delivering Dynamic Lectures in the College Classroom.*

John Orlando is the editor of *Online Classroom* newsletter. He helped build and direct distance learning programs at the University of Vermont and Norwich University, and has written more than 50 articles and delivered more than 40 presentations and keynotes on teaching with technology, online education, and social media. He is the associate director of the Faculty Resource Center at Northcentral University.

Crystal Ramsay is a research project manager of faculty programs at Penn State University.

Marie A. Revak is a faculty member at Jones International University. Previously, she taught at the United States Air Force Academy where she was twice given the Math Department Instructor of the Year award.

Patti Shank is the president of Learning Peaks LLC, an instructional design consulting firm. She was a contributing editor for *Online Learning Magazine,* is the co-author of *Making Sense of Online Learning,* and is the editor of *The Online Learning Idea Book.* She has a PhD in instructional design and is a Certified Performance Technologist.

Andrew Swanson is an instructional support specialist at Western Kentucky University.

Ann H. Taylor is the director of the Dutton e-Education Institute, College of Earth and Mineral Sciences, at Penn State University. She has worked in the field of distance education since 1991, focusing on learning design and faculty development.

John Thompson is associate professor in the computer information systems department at Buffalo State College.

Joan Thormann, PhD, is a professor in the division of Educational Technology at Lesley University. Since 1996, she has been developing and teaching courses online. Dr. Thormann has presented at more than 100 conferences nationally and internationally and has recently coauthored *The Complete Step-by-Step Guide to Designing and Teaching Online Courses* as well as other books about technology and education.

Scott Warnock, PhD, is an associate professor of English and director of the writing center at Drexel University. He is also author of *Teaching Writing Online: How and Why,* and he co-chairs the Conference on College Composition and Communication Committee for Best Practices in Online Writing Instruction.

Jennie Weber is an online instructor at Lake Region State College.

Maryellen Weimer has been the guiding hand and constant voice behind *The Teaching Professor* newsletter since 1987. She is an award-winning professor emerita of teaching and learning at Penn State Berks and won Penn State's Milton S. Eisenhower award for distinguished teaching in 2005. She has published several books, including *Inspired College Teaching: A Career-Long Resource for Professional Growth* (Jossey-Bass, 2010).

Lori Weir is program coordinator of information technology at Middlesex Community College.

Additional Resources

If you enjoyed this book, Magna Publications has additional resources for you:

BULK PURCHASES

To purchase multiple print copies of this book, please visit: www.MagnaGroupBooks.com

BOOKS

Teaching Strategies for the Online College Classroom:
A Collection of Articles for Faculty
https://www.amazon.com/Teaching-Strategies-Online-College-Classroom/dp/0912150483/
This book covers many topics relevant to both new-to-online and experienced online teachers, plus it includes references and recommended resources. It is a great starting place for anyone involved in the online learning community and anyone interested in improving their online offerings.

Essential Teaching Principles:
A Resource Collection for Adjunct Faculty
https://www.amazon.com/dp/B01HSEC0V2

This book provides a wealth of both research-driven and classroom-tested best practices to help adjuncts develop the knowledge and skills required to run a successful classroom

Grading Strategies for the College Classroom:
A Collection of Articles for Faculty
http://amzn.to/15RhFLX
This book provides insights into managing the complicated task of assigning a simple letter to a semester's work. It's a must-read for any faculty member seeking to understand how to use assessment to measure and enhance performance.

SUBSCRIPTIONS

Faculty Focus
www.facultyfocus.com
A free e-newsletter on effective teaching strategies for the college classroom, featuring a weekly blog post from Maryellen Weimer, PhD.

The Teaching Professor Newsletter
www.TeachingProfessorNewsletter.com
Published ten times a year, *The Teaching Professor* features ideas, insights, and best pedagogical practices written for and by educators who are passionate about teaching. Edited by Maryellen Weimer, PhD.

Online Classroom Newsletter
www.OnlineClassroomNewsletter.com
Published twelve times a year, *Online Classroom* helps you understand the current trends, challenges, ideas, and pedagogical insights for effective online instruction. Edited by John Orlando, PhD.

20-Minute Mentor Commons
http://bit.ly/2biCIR3
20-Minute Mentor Commons gives your entire campus unlimited, on-demand access to a library of Magna 20-Minute Mentor programs. This resource continues to grow as more programs are added regularly. They feature the top experts in higher education ready to answer pressing questions whenever, and wherever, your faculty need answers.

CONFERENCES

The Teaching Professor Conference
www.TeachingProfessor.com
This annual event provides an opportunity to learn effective pedagogical techniques, hear from leading teaching experts, and interact with colleagues committed to teaching and learning excellence.

The Teaching Professor Technology Conference
www.TeachingProfessorTechnologyConference.com
This conference examines the technologies that are changing the way teachers teach and students learn, while giving special emphasis to the pedagogically effective ways you can harness these new technologies in your courses and on your campus.

Made in the USA
Middletown, DE
27 October 2016